MEASURING YOUR LIBRARY'S VALUE

How to Do a Cost-Benefit Analysis for Your Public Library

DISCARD

Donald S. Elliott, Glen E. Holt, Sterling W. Hayden & Leslie Edmonds Holt

AMERICAN LIBRARY ASSOCIATION
Chicago   2007

While extensive effort has gone into ensuring the reliability of information appearing in this book, the publisher makes no warranty, express or implied, on the accuracy or reliability of the information, and does not assume and hereby disclaims any liability to any person for any loss or damage caused by errors or omissions in this publication.

Composition in New Caledonia and ITC Novarese using InDesign2 on a PC platform.

Printed on 50-pound white offset, a pH-neutral stock, and bound in 10-point cover stock by McNaughton & Gunn.

The paper used in this publication meets the minimum requirements of American National Standard for Information Sciences—Permanence of Paper for Printed Library Materials, ANSI Z39.48-1992. ∞

Library of Congress Cataloging-in-Publication Data

Measuring your library's value : how to do a cost-benefit analysis for your public library / Donald S. Elliott ... [et al.].
    p.   cm.
Includes bibliographical references and index.
ISBN 0-8389-0923-X (alk. paper)
1. Public libraries—United States—Cost effectiveness—Handbooks, manuals, etc. 2. Public libraries—Cost effectiveness—Handbooks, manuals, etc. 3. Public libraries—United States—Evaluation—Handbooks, manuals, etc. 4. Public libraries—Evaluation—Handbooks, manuals, etc. I. Elliott, Donald S.
Z731.M367 2007
025.1—dc22   2006019911

ISBN-10: 0-8389-0923-X
ISBN-13: 978-0-8389-0923-2

Printed in the United States of America

11 10 09 08 07   5 4 3 2 1

We dedicate this book in memoriam to our mothers—
Margaret Louise Elliott, Helen Schrader Holt,
and
Elizabeth Donovan Edmonds.
Our mothers recognized the benefits of teaching their children
to enjoy reading and libraries long before we set out on a decade
of research to measure such benefits.
Our research is but a small part of their legacy.

Dr. Donald S. Elliott
Dr. Glen E. Holt
Dr. Leslie Edmonds Holt

I dedicate this book to my wife and children,
who have provided inspiration and support
in our life's adventures.

Dr. Sterling W. Hayden

CONTENTS

ACKNOWLEDGMENTS   VII

1   Introduction to Cost-Benefit Analysis for Public Libraries   1

2   Fundamentals of Cost-Benefit Analysis   9

3   Important Considerations before Commissioning a CBA Study   28

4   Preparing to Measure Benefits   40

5   Measuring Library Benefits: Identifying and Sampling Library Users   54

6   Measuring Library Benefits: Preparing the Survey Instruments   69

7   Measuring Library Costs   89

8   Measuring Return to Taxpayer and Donor Investment in the Library   99

9   Wrapping Up Your Study: Communicating Your CBA Findings   111

10   Conclusions: Evaluating What Your CBA Study Accomplished   117

APPENDIXES

A   Measuring Consumer Surplus by Contingent Purchases of Substitutes: A Technical Appendix for Economists   125

B   Sampling Cardholders   127

C   Survey Instruments   132

D   Calculating and Reporting Survey Response Rates   159

E   Technical Insights for Project Consultants   166

GLOSSARY   175

INDEX   177

ACKNOWLEDGMENTS

WE THANK PLA, AND PARTICULARLY GEORGE NEEDHAM, NOW A VICE president at OCLC but formerly PLA's executive director, who encouraged us to ask for the critical funding that started this project. His encouragement and PLA's grant led to the pilot study at St. Louis Public Library and provided the experience we needed to launch the larger project.

We thank the Institute for Museum and Library Services and its staff for the two major grants that made the research for this project possible and for working with us to produce and test a tool that libraries can employ effectively.

We thank the St. Louis Public Library's board of directors, the staff, and its users. The library served as an alpha- and beta-site subject for our early research on cost-benefit analysis. Its directors, staff, and users offered criticism that helped us to refine our methodology. They also encouraged us in our work to measure and reveal the dollar value in their library's services.

We thank the directors and staff members of the thirteen libraries that aided us in the completion of our site studies. We especially thank the computer and data-processing staff at each of those institutions. They helped us process the patron records to create the databases that made our research possible.

We thank the many friends and colleagues from Southern Illinois University Edwardsville who supported our research. The university's Institute for Urban Research provided an academic home for our projects and conducted surveys used in two of the funded research projects. Professors Ralph Giacobbe and John Navin of the School of Business contributed to the design of survey instruments and databases used in our early research. Several graduate students from the Department of Economics and Finance, especially Christopher Dussold, Jullavut Kittiakarasakun, and Amonia Moore, assisted with literature searches, focus groups, empirical testing, and programming at different stages of our research.

Finally, we owe special thanks to Anne Watts, now manager of Machacek Branch in the St. Louis Public Library system. Anne provided invaluable assistance in helping us select good research sites and in devising and critiquing our initial research methodology.

CHAPTER 1

Introduction to Cost-Benefit Analysis for Public Libraries

PURPOSE OF THIS BOOK

If you are reading this book, you have more than a casual interest in determining the value of your library's service to its users. This book is designed for you. It is a how-to manual for those who want to prepare a statistical estimate of the benefits of their library's services to its customers.

Why do library professionals want to document the dollar value of their library's services? They want to make a strong case for their library. They want strong, convincing evidence to communicate the value of their library to government officials, board members, and donors. As one director exclaimed after seeing the result of his library's study, "Now we have a great sound bite!"

The libraries that participated in our demonstration studies found they could learn other important policy information as well. For example, cost-benefit analysis (CBA) can match the cost of a service with benefits from that service—in total and distributed across different user groups. It can show how ongoing users benefit from traditional services, like book checkouts, while the library gains new users from recent service innovations such as library computers and electronic databases. Understanding your customer base and its evolution is good business in any business, and libraries are no exception.

A couple of libraries used their demonstration study results to change staff training. One library, for example, dramatically increased the institution's in-service training budget because "investment in staff improvements would be seen immediately in increased benefits to users." Another director used the results to "Let . . . Staff Know

How Great They Are." In other words, the CBA study results were integrated into staff training with the specific intent of raising staff morale and reinforcing the importance of high-quality service.

We have no doubt that creative library managers will find many innovative ways to apply CBA results in their policy making and operations. The principal objective, however, remains a defensible estimate of the value of library services that will convince those whose opinions count in preserving or increasing library budgets.

Economists have long recognized cost-benefit analysis as an established tool to measure in dollar terms the benefits of public services like those libraries provide. Because of the research our team conducted with two major IMLS grants, we were able to test and retest our CBA methodology in numerous library settings. We know that the methodology we present in this book can be used to calculate defensible dollar estimates of benefits when used within the analytical limits we outline.

Not only is this a how-to book, it is also a communications primer. It provides illustrations of how you can tell your users, the general public, governance and budget officials, and possible donors about the direct benefits of your services. The methods that we suggest allow you to communicate those benefits for each annual tax dollar invested or as a rate of return on investment.

RESEARCH CHRONOLOGY

Our project began in a 1994 discussion of the Strategic Directions Committee of the Urban Libraries Council. During that discussion, the directors of a dozen urban libraries stated their need for a statistical methodology they could use to quantify the benefits of library services and communicate that value to elected officials, board members, donors, and their user constituents. One of the coprincipal researchers on this project, Glen Holt, agreed to try to develop the desired methodology.

The applied research project that grew out of that conversation lasted ten years, from 1994 through 2003. Staff members of the St. Louis Public Library (SLPL) and academic faculty from the School of Business at Southern Illinois University Edwardsville (SIUE) conducted the research. The timeline below describes the major phases of our research.

1994–1997:
St. Louis Public Library Case Study

The first two years of research were used to develop and apply cost-benefit analysis to SLPL as a prototypical case study. The SLPL study was partially funded by a grant from the PLA. The third year was spent refining the methodology, obtaining an IMLS grant, and finding partner libraries.

1997–2001:
Study of Five Large Library Systems

During this period, the team devised and executed CBA studies for the large public library systems of Baltimore, Maryland; Birmingham, Alabama; King County, Washington (the eastern suburbs of Seattle); and Phoenix, Arizona. At the same time, the team conducted a second study at SLPL, replicating the original case study but using improved methodology and obtaining results that confirmed the validity of the first study. These five systems were sufficiently different in size and the demographics of their service populations to allow a good test of the methodology. After the completion of this five-library study, the team reapplied and was awarded a second major research grant from IMLS for 2001–3.

2001–2003: Study of Nine
Medium-Sized and Smaller Library Systems

During these years, the team further refined its CBA methodology and applied it to three libraries in each of three different states. For the purpose of these nine demonstrations, the team defined medium-sized institutions as those serving a population between 50,000 and 150,000. Variation in the character of library service populations was a significant factor in selecting the nine participating libraries. By design, some systems invited to participate were mostly rural, others suburban, and still others exurban.

Socioeconomic differences were apparent as well. Some places were market towns dominated by retail and services. Some were manufacturing centers, and others were service centers using unskilled and semiskilled labor. Some had heavy concentrations of Hispanics, Asians, and a significant percentage of new immigrants or African Americans. Some were relatively wealthy, many were dominated by middle-income populations, and still others had populations that were predominantly poor.

To hold down travel costs, the team selected clusters of three libraries within or near three broadly defined metropolitan areas. The nine participating library systems were Joliet Public Library, Skokie Public Library, and Schaumburg Township District Library, all near Chicago, Illinois; Sterling Municipal Library, Montgomery County Memorial Library System, and Pasadena Public Library, all near Houston, Texas; and Everett Public Library, Mid-Columbia Library District, and Pierce County Library System, all near Seattle, Washington.

2003–2006: Data Compilation,
Analysis, and Writing

These fourteen library CBA studies produced volumes of statistical data. Processing that data, writing various IMLS reports, job changes for many team members, and proposing and writing this book for ALA has occupied our research time since the conclusion of the funded project.

KEEPING THE LIBRARY COMMUNITY INFORMED

Presentations

Throughout this project, we frequently reported the development of our methodology to the library profession in a variety of settings. Some reports were presentations; some were publications. Between 1997 and 2002, members of the team gave presentations to library association meetings and at CBA project libraries. Audiences at the latter often included staff, governance officials, and friends. Team members gave presentations in Alabama, Arizona, California (5), Colorado, Hawaii, Illinois (6), Kentucky, Maryland, Michigan, Minnesota, Missouri (3), North Carolina, Ohio (3), Oregon, Texas (6), Washington (5), and Wisconsin as well as in Australia, Egypt, Germany, New Zealand, and Singapore.

St. Louis CBA Project Publications

The team also published as the project developed. The evolution of the project preceding this book can be tracked back to its conception in the "Additional Reading" section at the end of this chapter.

RELIABILITY AND APPLICABILITY

The CBA methodology in this book was developed for use by large and medium-sized public libraries. We tested our methodology fifteen times on fourteen different library systems. As we expected, local variations increased when we moved our testing from large libraries to medium-sized and smaller libraries. When we examined systems with service area populations of less than 50,000 as possibilities for CBA applications, we encountered at least three types of problem.

First, there is the question of cost. Even the larger of the small public libraries in the United States have operating budgets that would be hard pressed to find the $15,000–$20,000 necessary to complete a basic study. These funds are required to hire expert help and to complete valid telephone or Web-based surveys with hundreds of individual library users.

Second, to obtain a valid survey, we asked data-processing staff of individual project libraries to pull random samples of 4,500 cardholders. Staff often had difficulty executing the random sampling. In addition, we often encountered a high incidence of record errors in the samples provided. We do not believe that database errors would be any less frequent in smaller library systems, which would make pulling a valid random sample problematic.

Third is the issue of privacy. From the outset, we conducted our research under SIUE Human Subject Research Guidelines. These guidelines held us to strict standards, including privacy, that have a basis in federal law. If we attempted to apply the CBA methodology we were testing to small libraries, we believed that the numbers of persons in some statistical cell categories might be so small as to make it possible for staff or even other users to identify individual persons.

To sum up, within the definitions we developed at the beginning of our research, we have developed a transportable, flexible CBA methodology to estimate the value of public library systems as small as those serving populations of about 50,000. We believe it is possible to survey libraries serving still smaller populations, but probably as statewide or regional service-valuation studies that could overcome some of the research issues we did not feel we could address in our studies. It will take time and money (and probably some persuasive politics) to ensure construction of a valid study in these statewide and regional settings, but we believe the findings could be worth the investment.

We certainly do not recommend easing the rigor of the methodology. Anyone expert in cost-benefit analysis will quickly detect when a methodology is relaxed, typically to obtain higher-value outcomes. At that point, the issue may move beyond something that is just academic to a significant public relations debacle in confronting critics who identify systemic overestimations of value.

POLICY IMPLICATIONS OF DOING A CBA STUDY

What Your Staff and Users Will Expect

Presumably you are considering a cost-benefit analysis in order to call positive attention to your library and its service operations. Studies like those described in this book do indeed provoke attention. And, like other types of analysis, planning, and evaluation, they often provoke fear—in both library staff and users.

The first policy implication of doing a CBA study, therefore, is that those executing the study need to communicate effectively with both staff and users about the nature and significance of the study. In today's cost-cutting, low-tax environment, staff and users alike may assume that any kind of study will lead to cuts in staff or service levels of favorite programs. Those doing the survey need to use both formal and informal channels to point out the rationale and possible benefits of every library study, especially one that estimates the benefits of services delivered to the public.

In addition to improvements in communications with staff and customers, the study results may lead to policy changes. CBA studies often reveal with extreme clarity the importance—or lack of importance—of benefits derived from certain services. The findings in our St. Louis CBA studies, for example, reinforced the importance of popular materials collections and demonstrated the low level of constituent interest in some of our specialized collections.

What You Should Expect from Your Cost-Benefit Analysis

When writer and radio personality Garrison Keillor completes his stories about the people of Lake Wobegon, one of the closing comments is that the community is a place where "all the children are above average." The library profession has not done much to offset a general communication tendency to lump classy libraries that make good use of their money to serve the needs of their constituencies with those that are strikingly mediocre or even worse.

This point is important because, when those who don't know much about CBA methodology first hear about cost-benefit analysis, they assume that all libraries will produce high benefits. Cost-benefit analysis, as we have applied it to libraries, discerns differences among libraries in the way they deliver services and, therefore, produce benefits. At the outset, we expected our studies of different libraries to find different levels of benefit. They did.

Before starting a CBA study, we have always advised libraries to be sure they want to do one. It is always possible that a study will determine that the library's benefits are valued *less* than the funding levels that support them. When this happens, it can yield a public relations problem for that library. We discuss other advantages and disadvantages of CBA studies as we take you through the research process.

Another characteristic of the CBA methodology explained in this book is that it is intentionally conservative in its estimate of value. Several of us on the research team have explained our methodology to groups of library professionals and found that our colleagues appreciate our determination not to overestimate the value of what we count and estimate. Frankly, it is easier to defend systematic undervaluations than obviously inflated overvaluations.

Finally, we add one more note of caution by way of introduction. We do not believe that those who use our methodology should attempt to make direct comparisons of benefits among different library systems, even those that seem quite similar on the surface. Our methodology applies cost-benefit analysis to estimate a defensible floor for the benefits provided by one library or by a whole library system. By intention, the estimates are conservative and may understate the value of the library. In some libraries, the undervaluation used to establish a floor may be substantial. In others, the undervaluation may not be as great, even when using a similar methodology. Because the exact amount of the undervaluation is not known, the results are not comparable across libraries.

OVERVIEW

Our goal in this book is to explain to readers how to do cost-benefit analysis in public libraries. The book will help you to learn about the methodology and to decide whether to attempt it or not. It will also help you recognize the perils and possibilities of using the methodology.

Even if you don't know much about statistics or economics, we hope that you find this book easy to read and to use as a reference. We begin with a general discussion illustrating the basic reasoning behind cost-benefit analysis. You will recognize this way of thinking almost immediately; each of us applies our own version of cost-benefit analysis many times every day. Next, the book covers critical considerations regarding why and how you might apply such an analysis in your own library. We even ask a series of questions to help you decide whether a CBA study is a good project for your library to undertake. Besides outlining how to design and execute a CBA study for your library, we include suggestions on how to summarize and defend the conclusions of your study, communicate results to special audiences, and use your study's results to accomplish strategic goals. A glossary is available for your reference should you encounter unfamiliar terms in later chapters. The documents and survey instruments we employed in our analyses are included in figures and the appendixes. We invite you to use them or modify them for your own CBA study.

A few of the more technical appendixes are intended for economists who assist in CBA projects, and these are labeled as such. Nevertheless, library professionals who take a special interest in the methodology may find these appendixes informative as well. Our recommended research procedures contain no "index numbers" or mystery calculations devised inside some black box or through use of a methodological "economic impact" hybrid that is not fully articulated so that readers may judge its rigor.

We wish you well in the CBA study you undertake. We hope you find it as rich in results and as informative as we did when we worked with so many of you to develop this application to libraries.

ADDITIONAL READING:
ST. LOUIS CBA PROJECT PUBLICATIONS
(MOST RECENT TO EARLIEST)

Holt, Glen E., Donald Elliott, Leslie Edmonds Holt, and Sterling Hayden. *Manual for Using Cost-Benefit Analysis to Value America's Medium-Sized and Smaller Public Libraries.* Published electronically in December 2005 on OCLC's Web Junction, www.webjunction.org.

Holt, Glen E., and Donald Elliott. "Measuring Outcomes: Applying Cost-Benefit Analysis to Middle-Sized and Smaller Public Libraries." *Library Trends* 51, no. 3 (2003): 424–40. (Themed issue, "Economics of Libraries," Louis G. Liu and Bryce Allen, issue eds.)

Holt, Glen E., and Donald Elliott. "Cost-Benefit Analysis: A Summary of the Methodology." *Bottom Line: Managing Library Finances* 15, no. 4 (2002): 154–58. (Feature article in a special issue, "Determining the Economic Benefits of Public Library Costs," written instead of author's regular quarterly column in this journal. Winner of best article for 2002.)

Holt, Glen E., and Donald Elliott. *Public Library Benefits Valuation Study.* Final report to the Institute of Museum and Library Services for National Leadership. Grant Number LL-80161-98, 1998–2000. St. Louis, MO: St. Louis Public Library, 2001. Published on IMLS website and at http://www.slpl.lib.mo.us/ libsrc/research.htm. (Reports and critiques project methodology on large public libraries in preparation for a second study replicating and refining the methodology using medium-sized and smaller libraries.)

Holt, Glen E., and Leslie Edmonds Holt. "Assessing the Value of Children's Library Services." *School Library Journal,* June 1999, 47.

Holt, Glen E., Donald Elliott, and Amonia Moore. "Placing a Value on Public Library Services." *Public Libraries* 38, no. 2 (1999): 98–108.

Holt, Glen E., and Donald Elliott. "Proving Your Library's Worth: A Test Case." *Library Journal* 123, no. 18 (1998): 42–44.

Holt, Glen E. "As Parents and Teachers See It: The Community Values of a Public Library." *Bottom Line: Managing Library Finances* 10, no. 1 (1997): 32–35.

Holt, Glen E., Donald Elliott, and Christopher Dussold. "A Framework for Evaluating Public Investment in Urban Libraries." *Bottom Line: Managing Library Finances* 9, no. 2 (1996): 4–13. (Feature article in a special issue, "Determining the Economic Benefits of Public Library Costs," written instead of author's regular quarterly column in this journal. Winner of best article for 1996.)

CHAPTER 2

Fundamentals
of Cost-Benefit
Analysis

SO YOU ARE ABOUT TO LEARN COST-BENEFIT ANALYSIS, ARE YOU? HOW brave you are. Sure sounds intimidating.

It's not. Honest. You are already an experienced practitioner of the art. All we need to do is help you see your library in the same evaluative framework you already use every day for personal and professional tasks. Once we have set up the framework, the rest of this book focuses on how to define, acquire, and interpret quantitative measures to flesh it out. Also, we give you some tips about how to communicate what you have discovered to people who are important to your library and its future. The conclusions of a CBA study are surprisingly easy to summarize and explain. They make great sound bites.

This chapter begins with a nontechnical explanation of cost-benefit analysis. Next, we contrast cost-benefit analysis with another often used economic tool, economic impact analysis, and explain when to use each. Most important, we outline a conceptual framework for estimating your library's value to the community. This framework can help you envision the benefits your library services provide to library users. We also present three alternative measures to communicate the value of your library to important public and constituent audiences. The chapter concludes with a discussion of the use of cost-benefit analysis to provide library outcome measures.

THE ECONOMIC BASIS OF COST-BENEFIT ANALYSIS

When we make decisions, each of us implicitly or explicitly weighs our options. We begin by defining a particular goal or objective. Next we identify alternative ways of reaching that goal. Each alternative typically offers us certain benefits, but at the expense of associated sacrifices or costs. We weigh how and how much we will benefit under each of the alternatives relative to what and how much we will have to sacrifice if we pursue that alternative. Having weighed the benefits and costs, we choose the option that provides the greatest net benefits—that is, the alternative with the greatest benefits relative to its costs.

For simple decisions, each of us follows this process almost intuitively. Suppose your goal is to retrieve your newspaper from a dark room. If you walk into a dark room, you have several options. You can walk in the dark, fumble for your newspaper, but risk stumbling and breaking something precious—possibly yourself. You can hesitate (but expend valuable time) to flick on a light switch, safely pick up your paper, then return, and flick the switch off. You might even consider a third strategy. You could take the time to find a flashlight first, gamble that it has fresh batteries, and walk into the room with the flashlight lit instead of using the light switch.

Which would you do? Many of us would turn on the lights rather than walk in the dark or get a flashlight because the benefits of that option are greatest relative to the cost, including our time and effort. Such decision making is so natural to us that we usually do it without any serious consideration. An economist's formal cost-benefit analysis follows the same logic but applies it in a structured way to more complex decisions.

Like individuals, communities must make decisions. Suppose that our community's goal is to provide a good place for its citizens to live—that is, to provide a good quality of life. Many different factors contribute to quality of life, so the community or its representatives must make choices. Should the community use its limited tax dollars to increase police protection, improve its schools, or expand its public library services? Should the community cut back expenses on two of these activities to do one? Or should it raise taxes so that it can do all three? A public policy economist will argue that the community should pursue the option or options that give the community the greatest benefits relative to cost. Cost-benefit analysis is a formal way of measuring the benefits of alternative public-sector options relative to the cost of those options.

Cost-benefit analysis has a long history of use in public-sector decision making. Analysts have applied cost-benefit analysis to such decisions as whether to construct a new dam, invest in K–12 and higher education, or offer public immunization and health services.[1]

Consider the decision whether or not to build a new lock and dam on the Mississippi River. Dams offer flood protection, recreation, and channel depth for barge navigation. Dams are also costly to build, maintain, and operate. By measuring the projected benefits from flood control, recreation, and barge transportation through a given future time period, economists can compare the benefits from the proposed dam with its costs and make recommendations regarding the construction of the dam.

In doing so, economists must be careful to identify and measure the appropriate benefits. Measuring the value of library services is accomplished in a similar way.

Direct and Indirect Benefits

Activities that we or our communities undertake can have both direct and indirect benefits. *Direct benefits* from a transaction or activity accrue to those individuals who are engaged immediately in the activity. For example, if you pay your physician for a flu shot to protect yourself from illness, you benefit directly in the form of reduced likelihood of getting the flu.

Your action also has *indirect benefits* for others. Because you are less likely to get the flu, you are also less likely to spread the flu to others. Hence, others benefit indirectly from your flu shot (but without sharing your pain and expense). Our community often encourages us, especially our children, to be immunized against certain diseases, not just for our own individual benefit but because the community as a whole benefits, too.

The combination of both significant direct and indirect benefits to members of the community relative to the cost of immunization often makes such public health programs a good investment for the community. That's how this nation eliminated polio, for example. Once public funds were used to support universal immunization against polio, this disease all but disappeared in the United States.

Similarly, public libraries provide both direct and indirect benefits. When a young girl participates in a summer reading program and maintains or improves her reading ability, she benefits directly. She enjoys her reading, learning, and participation in activities with others at the library. She develops strong reading skills that will help her in school and later in life.

Others in her community benefit from her participation, too, but indirectly. In a democracy, all of us benefit when voters have strong literacy skills and exercise them as an informed electorate. Furthermore, if the young girl grows to be a mother, she will pass her reading skills on to her children, benefiting not only them but also others in the community. Through the services they provide, libraries benefit patrons directly and others in the community indirectly.

To make good public-sector decisions, policymakers need to consider both direct and indirect benefits. A summer recreational youth baseball league may not only create happier and healthier teens (a direct benefit) but also reduce the incidence of vandalism and theft in a community (an indirect benefit to residents). Both direct and indirect benefits should be weighed against costs and are important in deciding if the community should provide support for such youth activities.

Indirect benefits are often much more difficult to identify and measure than direct benefits. Sometimes analysts may find it easy to identify and query direct beneficiaries but difficult to identify and query specific indirect beneficiaries. For example, libraries can readily identify some direct beneficiaries of their services, such as active cardholders or participants in summer reading programs. But some indirect beneficiaries, such as the future progeny of a young girl participating in the summer reading program, are not even born yet. Measuring the value of indirect benefits to current library users' future progeny would be expensive to undertake and difficult to execute. Surely the accuracy of the results would be open to challenge.

Economists have identified forms of *non-use benefits* that apply to some goods or services individuals do not use directly. *Existence value* refers to individuals' willingness to pay to support the existence or continuation of amenities like public libraries that they may never use themselves. Residents who do not use the library themselves may still value the existence of the library as an educational or social institution that improves the quality of life in their community. *Option value* refers to individuals' willingness to support the provision of a good or service on the chance that they may want to use it sometime in the future, even though they do not use it today.[2] Residents who do not use library services currently may value having a library in their community on the chance that they may wish to use it in the future. Measuring non-use benefits is difficult and produces results open to challenge.

Whether direct or indirect, clearly some benefits are more difficult to quantify than others. Some benefits are tangible—that is, conceptually identifiable and quantifiable. Others are intangible—that is, conceptually impossible (or at least impracticable) to quantify. Some, including non-use benefits such as existence and option value, are difficult and expensive to measure. Even if measured, the accuracy of such indirect measures is subject to challenge and difficult to defend.

Rather than attempt to quantify all benefits, economic analysts may choose to quantify only those they can measure and defend with confidence and merely catalog or describe those they cannot credibly measure. By measuring only some of the benefits, analysts intentionally underestimate overall benefits. Hence, the analysis is purposely conservative in its appraisal of benefits. With this conservative approach, when estimated benefits exceed costs, the audience for the study can have confidence that total benefits—including direct, indirect, tangible, and intangible benefits—will exceed costs by a greater (but unknown) amount. They can be confident that the activity under study is indeed worthy of undertaking or supporting.

In the methodology to evaluate public libraries outlined in this book, we are intentionally conservative. That is because we want librarians to be able to make a credible case for the value their libraries provide to their users. The worst thing library supporters can do with cost-benefit methods—or with any other measurement system—is to make exaggerated claims. Inevitably another knowledgeable library professional, an economist, or an informed citizen will dispute such exaggeration, hurting the library's credibility and standing in the community.

Cost-benefit analysis is a powerful tool for decision making because it measures both benefits and costs in dollars. Dollars of benefits can be weighed directly against dollars of costs to show clearly whether or not an activity is a worthy use of public tax dollars. One way of making this comparison is by constructing a ratio of benefits to costs. This ratio tells how many dollars of benefits the community receives per dollar of cost expended. A *benefit-cost ratio* (benefits divided by cost) is the public sector's analogue of the private-sector CEO's bottom line. If benefits are greater than costs, the ratio exceeds 1.0 and the project is a good use of community resources. If benefits are less than costs, the ratio is less than 1.0 and the community can find better uses for its resources. In other words, the benefit-cost ratio states whether or not the community is getting a good return for its investment. As we see later, this can be a very effective tool for conveying your library's CBA message to a wide variety of audiences.

DETERMINING A LIBRARY'S VALUE TO ITS COMMUNITY

Let's apply the concepts just discussed to public libraries. How can we identify, quantify, and communicate a library's value in dollars? How can we measure benefits? How might we measure costs? Relative to costs, are the benefits from the library's services sufficiently great to demonstrate that the library is a good investment of the community's resources?

Newspapers often carry stories about the regional economic importance of a new defense contract or loss of a professional sports team. Fiscal conservatives opposing tax levies and civic leaders who serve on boards of libraries and charitable foundations increasingly want hard numbers to show productivity, efficiency, and responsible stewardship of public resources. Which is a more appropriate tool to demonstrate the value of public libraries, cost-benefit analysis or economic impact analysis? Can these two tools be combined to measure the value an institution returns to its community?

Different Tools for Different Purposes: CBA and Economic Impact Analysis

Cost-benefit analysis should not be confused with *economic impact analysis*, another type of study often used to promote economic development or corporate investment. Economic impact analysis compares regional economic conditions in the presence of an activity versus regional economic conditions in that activity's absence. In other words, an economic impact study estimates the change in regional economic indicators, such as income and employment, resulting from the introduction or loss of the activity. Firms, economic development agencies, and even professional sports franchises often use economic impact studies to bolster support for their projects. For example, how much more employment, income, and local tax revenue would exist in a region if a new vehicle assembly plant or professional soccer team should locate there?

For acquisitions such as a vehicle assembly plant, the contributions to regional income, employment, and local tax revenues are usually impressive. By building vehicles that will be sold to purchasers outside of the region, the assembly plant will draw new revenues to the local economy that will fund new employment, income, and tax revenues. Not only will the assembly plant itself hire and pay many local workers (known as a direct impact), but local workers will spend their income in the local economy, creating additional jobs and income for others in the community. Thus, the direct impact of the auto assembly plant ripples through the local economy, magnifying the changes in employment, income, and local tax revenues.

Economists call this magnification a *multiplier effect.* Because of the multiplier effect, attracting a new vehicle assembly plant that employs a thousand workers may create several thousand jobs in the regional economy—impressive headlines in the local press. Economic development agencies and corporate interests often use such studies in publicity to muster public support for zoning variances, tax incentives, or relaxation of environmental regulations—changes that may be offered as a package to attract the assembly plant.[3]

Rarely is economic impact analysis an appropriate tool for measuring the contribution of a local cultural institution or public library to its community. It would be appropriate only if at least one of the following conditions were to apply:

> The institution attracts significant revenues from outside the region, such as grants, charitable contributions, state funding, or visitor spending.

> The presence of the institution locally permits residents to avoid purchases or travel to acquire similar services outside the region.

Major, unique cultural institutions such as Los Angeles's J. Paul Getty Museum or New York's American Museum of Natural History attract visitors from outside their regions. The visitors stimulate the region's economy with tourist dollars in the form of hotel, restaurant, and recreational purchases. In addition to attracting visitors to the region, such institutions also provide resident families with local recreational activities. Some resident families can choose to enjoy local cultural activities rather than vacation outside the region. The availability of these local cultural activities keeps these residents' dollars in the local economy rather than losing them to vacation resorts elsewhere. Keeping such spending at home stimulates the regional economy. Cultural institutions that attract visitors from outside the region and keep residents' dollars at home are likely to have a substantial economic impact. These institutions may find it advantageous to conduct economic impact studies for use in their community relations.

Similarly, libraries such as the New York Public Research Library or the Library of Congress have extensive historical holdings and unique research collections that attract visitors from outside their local service areas. Because individuals come to use them—or just to visit them—from outside the region, such libraries may have a substantial positive impact on the economies of their communities. Libraries that attract significant funding in the form of gifts or grants from outside their local service areas also may have a local economic impact.

Most public libraries, however, do not have such impacts. Most local public libraries do not attract substantial dollars to the local economy from outside the region. Most public libraries do not stem the leakage of dollars from the local economy by permitting residents to avoid purchases they would make elsewhere.

Almost all public libraries are locale serving, not visitor inducing. They are stewards of local financial support, tax revenues, charitable contributions, and grants. With these funds, libraries enhance the regional quality of life of the residents they serve. They educate, inspire, cultivate, and enchant local children, parents, seniors, and even business leaders who use library services. To devise a valid measure of these libraries' contributions to their communities, we must measure the value local residents place on the library's services and the value libraries contribute to the local quality of life. For such libraries, cost-benefit analysis, rather than economic impact analysis, is a more suitable technique for measuring the return to the community's investment.[4]

For an exceptional few public libraries or library systems, combining cost-benefit analysis and economic impact analysis may be an appropriate strategy. The New York Public Library contributes to the quality of life of local residents, attracts visitors to the city, and receives funding in the form of grants and contributions from outside the local region. Combining cost-benefit analysis and economic impact analysis is appropriate to measure its contribution to the New York area.

Using a similar rationale, the Seattle Public Library recently completed an "economic benefits assessment" for its new central library.[5] This carefully executed, conservative study offers many innovative perspectives and measures of the importance of the newly constructed central library to downtown Seattle. The study answers three important questions: the impact of the library on local businesses, how the new library has affected the economic and cultural vitality of downtown Seattle, and how it has affected Seattle's image to the outside world. This study should interest major urban central libraries, especially those that are contemplating or have recently completed major renovations or the introduction of new services.

Some statewide library systems may attract significant funding from outside their state and may have libraries with unique collections that attract visitors to the state. At the same time, these systems clearly serve the residents of their state. In such cases, combining cost-benefit analysis and economic impact analysis may be appropriate. Studies of statewide systems in Florida and South Carolina have employed combined methodologies.[6] For validity, such studies require careful design and execution to avoid overlap (double-counting) or survey bias that exaggerates the measure of benefits or impact reported.

In summary, when you set out to measure the value of your library to its community, select a measurement tool that best fits the circumstances of your institution and the question your audience wants answered. In short, pick the methodology that offers the best return to the dollars you will spend for the research study.

In most cases, the question you will want to answer for your board, patrons, grant agencies, city or county council, and electorate is "How much value does the library deliver to local residents relative to the local tax funding it receives?" If you serve primarily local residents, hire primarily local residents, and your funding is primarily local, then the additional insight you can gain from including an appropriately executed economic impact analysis is not likely to be worth the additional expense. Why? Your library will have negligible economic impact because you are collecting local dollars in taxes and then returning the dollars again to the local economy as wages and purchases. This does not expand the local economy in the same way a new auto plant would.

In the remaining discussion in this book, we assume that most libraries will not find economic impact analysis useful, and we focus on measuring direct benefits of library services.

A Framework for Public Library Cost-Benefit Analysis: The Service-User Matrix

To perform cost-benefit analysis for public libraries, researchers must credibly quantify in dollar terms both the value of the library's services to the community and the costs associated with those services. To structure the benefits component of the study, the researchers and the library's director (or project team) should always begin by reviewing the library's mission statement and its strategic, financial, and service plans. What are the primary types of user the library serves? What are the major categories of service the library provides? Which users are associated with which categories of service? To visualize these relationships and facilitate discussion, array the services and audiences in a *service-user matrix*. For example, we used a service-user matrix similar to that in table 2.1 in our IMLS-funded studies of five large urban libraries.[7] In this matrix, the major user groups (market segments) are "General users" (households), "Teachers" (educators), and "Businesses."

Because the study uses sample surveys to ascertain users' perceptions of value or benefit, select the service categories from the users' perspective, not by simply copying a list of the library's services. Don't think in terms of the library's current administrative or departmental structure, for example. Think instead about needs the users are attempting to satisfy and the library's services that satisfy those needs. For example, some libraries might distinguish between hard copy and electronic media and may even administer those with separate departments, budget lines, and personnel. From the users' perspective, however, reference material to use in a school term paper may come from either a reference text or a website. In asking the user about

TABLE 2.1
Typical service-user matrix

	GENERAL USERS	TEACHERS	BUSINESSES
Children's books	X	X	
Books for adults	X	X	
Videos/films	X	X	X
Audio/music	X		X
Magazines	X	X	X
Newspapers	X	X	X
Toys	X	X	
Parent-teacher materials	X	X	
Reference/research services	X	X	X
Special events	X	X	
Craft/activity programs	X	X	
Social skills/etiquette training	X		
Computer training	X	X	
Encyclopedias	X	X	
Dictionaries and almanacs	X	X	
Business and phone directories			X
Corporate reports			X
Government data/documents	X	X	X
Marketing or product data			X
Tax information	X		X
Financial information	X		X

value, it is not the media, department, or source that matters; it is whether the service satisfies the user's purpose.

Initially, the researchers and library director might identify a large number of user groups and align them with many detailed service categories. The more user groups surveyed separately in the study, however, the greater the number of survey interviews the study requires for statistical validity and the greater the cost of the study. Furthermore, the greater the number of service categories, the longer each survey interview and the lower the response rate and statistical performance of the survey. If an objective of the study is to explore the nature and distribution of benefits among different audiences, it is best to separate out and survey only the largest, most important user audiences, since the cost of surveys is proportional to the number of audiences classified and included in the survey.

For example, in addition to general users, teachers, and businesses, two other categories of library user might be government agencies and not-for-profit organizations (other than educational organizations). In our experience, the number of library patrons in these categories, their response rates, and the difficulty of surveying these users make the costs of including them disproportionately high relative to the benefit value measured, even for large urban libraries. To hold down the costs of the surveys we have executed, we excluded government agencies and not-for-profit organizations as user categories. By excluding them, we did not capture most of the benefits accruing to these two groups in our studies. Thus, these estimates of libraries' value were somewhat understated; that is, the results were conservative.

Table 2.2, the service-user matrix in our IMLS-funded studies of medium-sized and smaller public libraries, further illustrates user groups. Note that in these studies only general users and teachers were included. Even in large urban libraries, business use accounted for only 6 percent (King County, Washington) to 22 percent (Phoenix, Arizona) of total benefits to all direct users. For smaller libraries, benefits from use by businesses are likely to be negligible (and therefore not worth the expense to measure) relative to use by households and educators. To reduce costs of the studies of medium-sized and smaller libraries, we surveyed only households and educators and reported separate estimates of value for only those two groups. Also note in table 2.2 that the categorization of services for medium-sized and smaller libraries is less extensive and detailed than in the table 2.1 service-user matrix. This change reduces the length of survey interviews and enhances response rates and statistical confidence in the conclusions of the analysis.

Alternative Measures of Benefits

Economists have many different ways of measuring benefits from a service or activity. Among these are consumer surplus and contingent valuation analysis.[8]

Consumer Surplus

Economists often use consumer surplus in policy studies. *Consumer surplus* represents the monetary value consumers associate with a good or service in excess of any costs they incur to get it. For example, when purchasing a vehicle, the buyer often has a maximum outlay in mind and will spend no more than that amount. After successfully negotiating a price, the buyer may think "Wow! I got a really great deal. I would have been willing to pay more but didn't have to do so!" The extra value the buyer experiences but does not have to pay is the car buyer's consumer surplus.

Patrons of a public library service experience consumer surplus, especially since most library services are free of fees, whereas a similar service from a private vendor would carry a significant price. Although most library services are free in the sense

TABLE 2.2
Sample service-user matrix for medium-sized and smaller libraries

	HOUSEHOLDS	TEACHERS
Staff help		X
Information	X	
Tutoring	X	
Magazines and newspapers		X
Magazines		
English-language	X	
Foreign-language	X	
Newspapers		
English-language	X	
Foreign-language	X	
Computers		X
General use	X	
High-speed Internet	X	
Software	X	
Classes	X	
Reference		
Electronic reference		X
Periodical articles	X	
Scientific and professional journals	X	
Business and investment	X	
Genealogy	X	
Encyclopedias		X
Hardbound	X	
CD/DVD	X	
Adult services		X
Books	X	
Programs	X	
Children's services		X
Books	X	
Programs	X	
Audiovisual		X
Music	X	
Video	X	
Books on tape or disk	X	

that libraries charge no explicit price, patrons do expend effort and time to access the services. This time and effort are an implicit price to the patron. The value of the benefits patrons receive above and beyond this implicit price is the patrons' consumer surplus associated with the service.

One way of measuring the consumer surplus associated with a particular good or service uses information about patrons' willingness to pay for similar goods or services. You may be aware of an analogous practice. Real estate agents or property appraisers who evaluate houses not currently offered for sale often base their appraisals on recent sale prices of comparable properties. Economists can acquire and apply similar data to measure the value associated with an array of library services.

Private booksellers, music stores, video rental agencies, and online sites offer many close substitutes for library services. For example, rather than borrowing children's books from their local library, households could buy them online or from their local bookseller. Businesses could subscribe to online database or research services rather than send a staff member to the local library to obtain data for a marketing study.

By measuring how much a household uses the library's children's books, how much the household currently spends for children's books from private vendors, and how much the household would spend for children's books from private vendors if children's books were not available from the library, an economist can estimate the dollar value of the household's consumer surplus derived from using library children's books. (See appendix A for a technical defense of this method.) Similarly, by measuring a business's use of library databases and asking how much the business would spend to access similar databases if they were not available from the library, an economist can estimate the dollar value of benefits to the local business from using library database services.

Typical questions in our surveys of a random sample of library users ask a library's patrons how many books they borrow from the library during a typical month, how many books they buy, and how many additional books they would buy if they could not borrow books from their local library. From their responses, one can estimate the value library patrons place on the privilege of borrowing books in excess of any cost of accessing the library.

Researchers estimate consumer surplus for each library service used by each patron surveyed, then add up these dollar estimates for all respondents for each library service. From this measure, they extrapolate the sample totals to the population of all library users. An important precaution taken as a part of that extrapolation is testing the sample characteristics of those responding to the survey against the characteristics of the population as a whole. Correcting for any bias in the sample of patrons responding to the survey as opposed to the population as a whole makes the estimate of the consumer surplus much more accurate and defensible. When completed, this process provides an estimate of total direct annual benefits for that library service measured in dollars. Summing the resulting figures for all library services provides an estimate of total direct annual benefits for all library services.

Contingent Valuation

Rather than measure consumer surplus through the purchase of alternative substitutes, researchers can ask consumers directly about their willingness to exchange a good or service or a bundle of goods and services. This type of measurement is known as *contingent valuation analysis.*

Researchers have used contingent valuation measures extensively, even in judicial proceedings, to evaluate environmental conditions. For example, expert witnesses provided contingent valuation measures in controversial testimony in litigation to determine environmental damages charged in the 1989 oil spill by the *Exxon Valdez* in Prince William Sound.[9]

Two alternative measures of contingent valuation are available, although one is considered more reliable than the other. The "willingness-to-pay" (WTP) approach asks respondents how much they would be willing to pay to get something they do not have. The "willingness-to-accept" (WTA) approach asks respondents how much they would accept to give up something they already have. Generally, WTA estimates of value are greater than WTP estimates and are considered less reliable.

In our own, conservative CBA research, we measure the value of a library to its community only in terms of benefits to library users, and we now employ only the WTP method of contingent valuation. Alternatively, Svanhild Aabo, in her national CBA study of the Norwegian library system, set as her objective to measure both use and non-use values, so her sample of households included both library users and non-users.[10] Her survey measured citizens' WTP and WTA to maintain their system of public libraries by adding library CBA questions to a recurring nationwide survey of Norwegian citizens conducted as personal interviews in the respondents' homes. Because she used personal interviews with extensive follow-up questions, Professor Aabo defends her WTA estimates (four times greater than WTP) as providing reliable, useful CBA measures. She argues that WTA estimates are the appropriate theoretical measure because respondents view library access as something they already are entitled to have. Nevertheless, using personal interviews to conduct surveys would not be feasible in most CBA studies for individual libraries, like those we discuss in this book, because personal interviews of randomly selected households are prohibitively expensive.

In our early CBA studies of five large urban libraries, interviewers asked library cardholders both WTA and WTP questions.[11] The WTA question for general users was as follows:

> Suppose that in the next election the ballot contained a referendum on closing all public libraries. The referendum states that all public libraries will close, and the budgetary savings will be used to lower taxes or provide annual cash payments to households. Under these circumstances, would you vote to close the libraries if the yearly tax savings or cash payments to your household were an amount ranging from $__ to $__?

Researchers randomly assigned predetermined payback ranges varying from "$1 to $100" to "over $2,500" to the blanks in the question.

Librarians will smile knowingly when we tell them that most respondents were unwilling to close their libraries at any reasonable price. Those who were unwilling to close their libraries regardless of the amount offered were asked a follow-up question:

> Why would you vote "NO" to closing public libraries regardless of tax savings
> or cash payments to your household?

Their answers reflected widely spread, sincere appreciation that the library is an important social institution contributing to their community in many ways. Although these responses validate many perceptions of libraries' roles and provide wonderful supporting anecdotes for directors' luncheon speeches, the survey responses could not provide statistically reliable estimates of a library's value in conservative dollar terms—the primary objective of a CBA study. To conserve on interview time and cost, we excluded WTA questions from our subsequent CBA studies. We recommend that those who attempt contingent valuation studies for their individual libraries not use WTA. It is not likely to provide dollar estimates of benefits that can be used in any defensible manner.

In our studies of large urban libraries, the WTP question for general users was as follows:

> Suppose that no libraries had ever existed and taxes for libraries had never
> existed. How many dollars of taxes or fees would your household be willing
> to pay annually to create and maintain your library as it exists today?

Respondents rounded their answers to the nearest $100.

In subsequent studies, we have tried to make the hypothetical scenario more realistic than telling respondents to assume that libraries never existed. Instead, we begin our question by describing a scenario in which their library is destroyed by fire, storm, or some other natural disaster and is not covered by insurance. The question for general users goes on to ask about their support for a referendum to rebuild and maintain the library as it existed before its destruction.

Our response rates to this question have been good. Typically, the resulting WTP estimates of libraries' value to their community are the most conservative of the valuation estimates we have used and the ones participating libraries have used when they provided CBA information to their constituents.

Value of Time

A third method of evaluating library benefits borrows from a technique long used by environmental economists to measure the value of recreational resources such as national parks and forests. The premise is that the value of the benefits users receive must be at least as great as the value of the time and effort the users expend. Thus, by asking park visitors about their travel plans and outlays, researchers can establish a lower limit on the value visitors place on their vacation at the park. Applying the same argument to library services, researchers measure the value of the time, travel, and other outlays library patrons expend in using library resources. This technique was prominent in a recent CBA study of Florida's library system; the researchers in that study call this measure *user investment*.[12]

In our own studies of major urban libraries, interviewers applied this method by asking households about the time and travel they spent using library services.[13] For respondents who provided income information, the researchers evaluated time spent using the library on the basis of the income figures provided. To ensure that estimates were conservative, they evaluated time spent by stay-at-home spouses and teens at rates below minimum wage and placed no value on time of preteen children.

We have several reservations about this method as a valid measure of the value of a library to its community and no longer use it in our CBA studies. First, it is important to remember that patrons' time and effort expended in accessing library services is a cost, not a benefit.[14] Economists call the time and effort associated with searching and accessing a good or service *transaction costs*.

Although it is true that the benefits of the services users receive must be at least as great as the costs the users expend to access them, from the community's perspective it is the net benefits to users and community that really matter. Time and effort expended in accessing library services are as much a cost to the community as the tax support the community provides. Thus, the net benefits to the community would be zero if benefits were measured solely in this manner.

Alternatively, if accessing library services is less costly to users than other means to achieve the same ends, then the cost savings to library users is a benefit and part of the value of the library to the community. For example, if it is simpler and more convenient for a user to access a source at the local library than to search and order the materials from Amazon.com, then the user benefits and this contributes to the value of the library to the community. The role of a library as a place for one-stop shopping for many types of information strengthens this convenience factor and boosts library benefits. In the recent Florida library CBA study, the researchers measured the net benefit the Florida libraries provide by reducing transaction costs.[15]

Another problem with using the value of time as an evaluative measure is the difficulty of evaluating users' time realistically. For breadwinners, should recreational time be valued differently from work time? How should one evaluate the time and services of a stay-at-home spouse? Of a senior citizen? Of a child? The economics literature addresses some of these issues in applications such as CBA studies of mass transit systems and in testimony for personal injury litigation, but these measurements are controversial. To measure the benefits of using library services, we favor the consumer surplus and contingent valuation techniques over user investment of time.

Outcome Measures

In mustering support and defending existing budgets and practices, library directors must address many different audiences—both external and internal. Some audiences, especially mayors, councils, governing boards, taxpayer organizations, and grant agencies, are concerned primarily about funding levels and budgets. Some audiences, including governing boards, friends groups, and foundations, are concerned about the library's effectiveness in serving the community. Some audiences, especially administrators and staff, are concerned about allocation of resources among services within the library, staff morale, and management priorities. Cost-benefit analysis can provide measures and information helpful in addressing all of these audiences.

A CBA study provides summary measures that show the library's efficiency in using taxpayer funding. By measuring benefits in dollar terms and comparing them to funding, CBA results show how the community estimates the value of the library relative to its tax support. A typical study conclusion might read like this: "For every dollar of annual local taxpayer support, the library returns $2 of benefits to local library users." In addition, by comparing the stream of net benefits (annual benefits less annual operating costs) with the value of library assets, the study might also conclude this: "The library returns 20 percent in benefits annually for the community's investment in library buildings and collections." Such conclusions from a CBA study offer impressive communication points for anyone soliciting support for a tax referendum, assuring a grant agency of the library's efficient use of funds, or defending a library's budget against fiscal attack.

A CBA study can show how the library serves the community and supports important constituent groups, such as educational institutions and businesses. In the service-user matrix, researchers can design the study to identify benefits by user group. For example, a CBA study can show how the library's benefits to the community are distributed among general users, educators and their students, and local businesses. Our CBA studies of many libraries document the impressive importance of the local library as a partner in the education of the community's children.

A CBA study can also help the library director and administrative staff analyze the appropriate allocation of the library's budget among library services, set priorities in strategic planning, and provide patron feedback to library staff that often bolsters staff morale. Such studies can demonstrate in rich detail how the public values different services. By reviewing the contributions to benefits by different services, the library administration can gain insight into whether some services should receive more funding or less funding, or whether some services should be promoted to ensure that the public is fully aware of their availability and usefulness.

Our CBA studies have always included an opportunity for respondents to offer comments to the library director. In rare cases, comments regarding staff may alert the director to situations for which counseling or professional development is appropriate. More often, however, such comments have complimented the library staff for their courtesy, effort, and expertise. Library directors pass these comments on to staff collectively or, in some cases, by department or individual. In all cases, the reported impact on staff morale has been positive and significant.

Clearly, as an outcome measure, cost-benefit analysis contrasts a measure of output (benefits to users and the community) with a measure of input (cost). Because the focus is on output per dollar of input, cost-benefit analysis gauges the efficiency with which a library uses public funds.

We never suggest that a CBA study should replace other established forms of communication librarians find effective. If traditional library communication tools work for you, by all means continue using them with the audiences for which they are effective. However, in a competitive resource climate or in front of a fiscally conservative audience of government officials or possible donors, a well-crafted direct comparison of dollar benefits and dollar costs may leave a more lasting impression than multiple anecdotes about children and new immigrants reading at the library.

How does cost-benefit analysis differ from another tool—the HAPLR ratings?[16] Clearly the HAPLR ratings are intended for comparative purposes. Unlike the HAPLR ratings, however, the results of CBA studies are not useful for comparing libraries. Our CBA studies are tailored to individual libraries or library systems. Their results are purposely conservative and understate the true value of a library's benefits to the community. Some libraries' studies may be based on more conservative assumptions and measurements than others. For these and other reasons, comparing the results of CBA studies across libraries is likely to be misleading and contentious.

SUMMARY

Cost-benefit analysis is an economic tool that libraries can use to measure the monetary value of the library to the community relative to the investment the community has made in the library either year by year or cumulatively over many years through its investment in collections, equipment, and buildings. Of several alternative ways of measuring the value of a library's services, we advocate two that have worked well for a broad spectrum of libraries. One is the consumer surplus approach, in which patrons evaluate library services relative to alternative market services they could purchase. The second, a form of contingent valuation analysis, evaluates the existence of the library in its entirety using a measure of respondents' willingness to pay.

The overwhelming majority of library directors who participated in our IMLS-funded CBA demonstration projects have found the studies useful in a variety of ways. Library directors can use the conclusions of a CBA study to address many audiences: taxpayers and citizens, superior taxing jurisdictions or levels of government to which the library reports, the library board, external grant agencies and foundations, and internal administrators and staff. A CBA study can provide impressive sound bites relating to the community's return on investment or rich detail describing the distribution of benefits by service or user group. Whether the priority is improved public relations or more efficient management of resources, a CBA study can assist the library in carrying out its mission and reaching its goals.

NOTES

1. Edward M. Gramlich offers a useful primer with many examples of applications and a more formal presentation of the topic; see Gramlich, *A Guide to Benefit-Cost Analysis*, 2nd ed. (Englewood Cliffs, NJ: Prentice-Hall, 1990).

2. See the discussion of non-use valuation in Joseph Breedlove, *RL30242: Natural Resources: Assessing Nonmarket Values through Contingent Valuation* (CRS Report for Congress, June 21, 1999), available at http://www.ncseonline.org/NLE/CRSreports/Natural/nrgen-24 .cfm?&CFID=16645991&CFTOKEN=7270383#Nonuse%20Values.

3. For a discussion of similar examples of the economic impacts of institutions of higher education, see R. Beck, D. Elliott, J. Meisel, and M. Wagner, "Methodological Issues in Economic Impact Studies of Regional Colleges and Universities," *Growth and Change* 26, no. 2 (1988): 17–33. Many of the same concerns raised in this article apply to the application of economic impact analysis to local or regional public libraries.

4. Glen E. Holt, Donald Elliott, and Christopher Dussold, "A Framework for Evaluating Public Investment in Urban Libraries," *Bottom Line: Managing Library Finances* 9, no. 2 (1996): 4–13.

5. Berk and Associates, *The Seattle Public Library Central Library: Economic Benefits Assessment: The Transformative Power of a Library to Redefine Learning, Community, and Economic Development* (Seattle, WA: Seattle Public Library, July 2005), available at http://www.spl.org/pdfs/ SPLCentral_Library_Economic_Impacts.pdf.

6. José-Marie Griffiths, Donald W. King, and Thomas Lynch, *Taxpayer Return on Investment in Florida Public Libraries: Summary Report* (Tallahassee: State Library and Archives of Florida, 2004), available at http://dlis.dos.state.fl.us/bld/roi/pdfs/ROISummaryReport.pdf; and Daniel D. Barron, Robert V. Williams, Stephen Bajjaly, Jennifer Arns, and Steven Wilson, *South Carolina Public Library Economic Impact Study* (Columbia: University of South Carolina, January 2005), available at http://www.libsci.sc.edu/SCEIS/home.htm.

7. Glen E. Holt, Donald Elliott, and Amonia Moore, "Placing a Value on Public Library Services," *Public Libraries* 38, no. 2 (1999): 98–108.

8. Holt, Elliott, and Moore, "Placing a Value on Public Library Services."

9. See, for example, Richard T. Carson, Robert C. Mitchell, W. Michael Hanemann, Raymond J. Kopp, Stanley Presser, and Paul A. Ruud, "Contingent Valuation and Lost Passive Use: Damages from the Exxon Valdez," available at http://www.rff.org/~kopp/working_papers/qe94-18.pdf; and *Economic, Social, and Human Impacts: A Selected Bibliography on the Exxon Valdez Oil Spill* (March 2002), available at http://www.evostc.state.ak.us/History/Downloadables/biblio_social .pdf. For an overview of contingent valuation and its applications and critiques, see Paul R. Portney, "The Contingent Valuation Debate: Why Economists Should Care," *Journal of Economic Perspectives* 8, no. 4 (1994): 3–17; and Breedlove, *RL30242: Natural Resources*.

10. Svanhild Aabo, "Valuing the Benefits of Public Libraries," *Information Economics and Policy* 17, no. 2 (2005): 175–98, available at http://dx.doi.org/doi:10.1016/j.infoecopol.2004.05.003.

11. Holt, Elliott, and Moore, "Placing a Value on Public Library Services," 106.

12. Griffiths, King, and Lynch, *Taxpayer Return on Investment in Florida Public Libraries.*

13. Holt, Elliott, and Moore, "Placing a Value on Public Library Services."

14. See Bruce R. Kingma, *The Economics of Information* (Englewood, CO: Libraries Unlimited, 1996), chap. 11.

15. Griffiths, King, and Lynch, *Taxpayer Return on Investment in Florida Public Libraries.*

16. Thomas J. Hennen Jr., *Hennen's American Public Library Ratings for 2004* (2004), available at http://www.haplr-index.com/HAPLR2005AmericanLibraries.htm.

CHAPTER 3

Important Considerations
before Commissioning
a CBA Study

A WELL-EXECUTED CBA STUDY CAN BE USEFUL IN MANY WAYS. UNLESS donated, however, it costs money, time, and effort. If you replicate our methodology, the cost probably is at least $15,000 for a basic study. Moreover, it may reveal troubling issues concerning your library's operation that you have not previously addressed. Before commissioning a study, therefore, pause and reflect:

- Review carefully what you want the study to accomplish.
- Assess whether the study is feasible.
- Calculate the budget and staff resources you can afford to devote to the study.
- Decide how optimistic you are regarding the study's outcomes and conclusions.

This chapter outlines questions to ask in deciding whether or not to undertake a CBA study for your library and how to frame the study so that the analysis is tailored to your institution and accomplishes what you intend.

REASONS TO UNDERTAKE A CBA STUDY

Consider carefully why *your* library should undertake a CBA study. What positive contributions could this kind of analysis make in accomplishing your library's mission and goals? Are there possible negative outcomes from executing a study?

Defend Your Library's Current Funding

Ironically, the most urgent reason for expending funds and resources on a CBA study is to make a better case in defense of your library's funding. When competing for budget funds or taxpayer support, organizations that can document their contributions to community welfare are more likely to retain the funds they need to survive and to move forward. Increasingly, fiscal conservatives are asking for defensible, hard-dollar figures that show the community's rate of return for each tax dollar entrusted to your library's care.

ASK: Are my library's current operations or financial future threatened by monetary problems? If so, will fiscal decision makers respond positively to credible, defensible information that shows the value of benefits the library provides to the community and the library's responsible stewardship of public funds?

Promote Your Library's Case for Increased Funding

A second strategic reason for commissioning a CBA study is to make the case for increased funding to expand library services or the facilities and technology that enable those services. In a capital campaign, what better way to solicit taxpayers, foundations, government officials, or individual donors than to show that each dollar invested in the library provides an impressive rate of return in benefits to the community? In a tax referendum to enhance operating funds, sound bites that address the dollar value of the library to the community can complement heart-tugging anecdotes and photographic images used to make the appeal.

ASK: Is my library preparing a capital campaign or request for additional operating funds? If so, will taxpayers, foundations, and donors respond positively to credible, defensible information that shows that each dollar invested in the library provides an impressive return in benefits to the community?

Demonstrate Responsible Stewardship of Public Funds

Responsible stewardship of public funds requires a library director to manage the library to maximize the benefits it provides to the community. The rich detail provided by a CBA study can assist library friends, board members, and staff to allocate resources more effectively to match users' preferences, identify niche markets that the library should serve well, and target marketing campaigns to inform and educate users about underutilized library services.

ASK: In allocating my library's budget, would it be helpful to know how much users value different library services? Would I find information regarding the distribution of benefits across specific user groups, niche markets, or geographic areas helpful in planning and allocating operating resources?

REASONS NOT TO UNDERTAKE A CBA STUDY

Disgruntled Patrons

By its very nature a library CBA study will attract public attention and comment. The CBA strategy outlined in this book gives your users a real (i.e., a statistically valid) opportunity to tell interviewers what they think of your services. Through the process of the study, hundreds of patrons involved in the survey will be asked their opinions about library services as they understand and use them. A library that has disgruntled patrons who are upset with staff, hours, or service levels will find that those user frustrations color CBA conclusions and survey comments. In addition, for credibility, an outside agency such as a university or professional consulting firm will be conducting the study. Once the study is under way, you will find it difficult to control the outcome or hide the results.

Small Library Size

Are some libraries more likely to find favorable results from a CBA study than others? Of course. As suggested in chapter 2, the reason for using cost-benefit analysis is that it validates performance levels.

Library characteristics—some outside the director's control—can affect performance. In our experience, larger libraries with large cardholder populations often have higher returns per dollar of tax support than smaller libraries, in part because of economies of scale; in other words, size matters. Efficient operating costs do not appear to rise proportionally with cardholder population and collection size. Thus, benefit-cost ratios for well-managed larger libraries tend to be higher, in general, than those for well-managed smaller libraries. Larger libraries also are more likely to be able to accommodate the expense and technological requirements associated with a CBA study.

ASK: How confident am I that my library serves the community well for the fiscal support that it receives? Might a CBA study suggest that my library does not provide community benefits at least as great as its community tax support?

Challenging Database Requirements

The CBA methodology outlined in this book requires individual—but identity-protected—surveying of cardholders. A library that does not clean and update its cardholder information regularly (for our research purposes, at least once every three years) or one with a weak or overburdened IT staff may not be capable of executing a defensible CBA study.

To ensure credibility, researchers must identify and count those patrons who have used the library during the past twelve months. For general users, the IT staff must condense the cardholder database by collapsing cards with the same addresses or phone numbers. In this way, the database becomes a directory of library-using households rather than individual cardholders—a "filtered" database. If address or phone information in cardholder records is outdated, incomplete, or formatted or coded inconsistently, the library cannot conduct valid user sampling and surveys. Following the instruction of the researchers, the IT staff of the library must draw a stratified random sample (explained fully in chapter 5) of library-using households and provide it and associated cardholder information to the researchers in a timely fashion.

We cannot overemphasize the importance of obtaining accurate user counts and conducting valid sampling. Because only a fraction of users respond to surveys, researchers must extrapolate the benefits accruing to those representative respondents to find the total benefits to all active users. If the count of active users is unreliable or the sample of respondents is biased, the conclusions regarding benefits to all active users or to the community generally are neither credible nor defensible. Any expenditure and effort invested in such a study is in vain.

> ASK: How current and complete are my library's cardholder records? Do the records include valid phone numbers and addresses consistently formatted and reliably coded? Is my library IT staff capable of following researchers' instructions to filter the cardholder database and select a stratified random sample?

Often a library will identify more than one class of user in its service-user matrix. In addition to general users, the library may wish separate information regarding use by other groups such as educators or businesses. If so, the library and researchers must be able to identify, count, and sample record bases, directories, or lists of active users in each of these groups.

> ASK: How important is separate information regarding special user groups to the goals of my CBA study? Is it reasonable to expect the library staff to identify, count, and sample active users in each of the groups?

Cost of the Study

A significant consideration in deciding to undertake a CBA study is cost. Expect a CBA study to cost at least $15,000 (in 2006 dollars), depending on its scope and timing. Extensive, detailed studies at larger libraries may cost substantially more. The out-of-pocket cost of a CBA study consists primarily of payments to engage an external research consultant and contract fees for a survey agency to collect and process data. In addition, the study requires commitment of internal library resources to assist with study design, sampling, execution, and publicity.

To conduct a credible CBA study, hire an objective external researcher. Most regional colleges and universities have economists on their faculties who can supervise this type of study. Other such specialists sometimes reside on the staff of state agencies such as economic development departments. Expect to pay at least $5,000 for a consultant, depending on the timing and scope of your study.

Your research consultant may assist you in selecting a survey agency to conduct the interviews with library users. The cost of surveys depends on the number of user groups about which you want separate information, the mode of survey (e.g., Web-based, phone, or both), and the length and complexity of your survey instruments. The cost can also vary with the timeline you set for the study. In chapter 4 we review points to consider in hiring a research consultant and a survey agency.

In addition to the expense of hiring a researcher and survey agency, you and your staff must spend considerable time working with the researcher to tailor the study, cleaning and sampling user databases, assembling cost data, and acting on the study's results. Consider whether you and your staff can afford the commitment of time and effort that a CBA study requires.

> ASK: How much of my library's funds and resources am I willing to devote to a CBA study? What timeline must the study meet to serve my goals?

DESIGNING YOUR CBA STUDY

Frame the Benefits Side of Your Study

Begin by considering how you will use the results of the study. If its sole purpose is to provide credible, defensible sound bites in a publicity campaign to ward off threatened closure, fend off budget cuts, or solicit taxpayer and donor support, then the study design and sampling can be relatively simple and the cost of the study restrained.

Simplest Study

For this type of study, sample the filtered cardholder database representing households, let respondents self-identify their user group, and restrict the survey instrument to questions that solicit user characteristics and willingness to pay to preserve the library in its current state. A computer-assisted telephone survey instrument (sometimes called CATI) or Web-based survey instrument can branch to WTP questions tailored to the user groups self-identified by the respondent.

For example, suppose that a household representative responds that a teacher resides there. Then, in addition to a WTP question addressing the household's general use, the researcher can design the instrument to solicit willingness to pay to preserve library educational services. A question might ask the teacher to estimate the amount of money that her/his school would have to spend annually to preserve the quality of education if neither the teacher nor the teacher's pupils could use the public library.

Detailed Study

Some libraries may seek more detailed information than the procedures outlined above can provide. For example, you may wish your study to provide not only credible, defensible information regarding the value of the library to the community as a whole but also information that details the value of benefits associated with individual library services or specific user groups. Use your library's mission statement and goals to consider the major categories of service the library provides and the specific user groups about which you want separate information. Array these visually in a service-user matrix, as described in chapter 2. Mark the cells in the matrix that match each service with the user groups most likely to use and value that service. For each matrix cell, the survey instrument should contain a separate set of queries to measure the value of the corresponding service to the designated user group.

> ASK: How much detail do I require to meet the purpose of my study? Do I need only general sound bites about the library's value to the community relative to its fiscal support? Or, in addition to the library's value to the community, do I need specific information about benefits from individual services or to separate user groups?

Frame the Cost Side of Your Study

In conveying the value of the library to the community, a cost-benefit analysis compares the value of the benefits the community receives with the costs associated with the library. There are several different ways of making this comparison. One method focuses on the annual flow of library services to the community and the operating cost associated with providing the services while sustaining the library's buildings, collections, and equipment. A second method recognizes that a library is a cultural legacy built over many generations. A library—its buildings, collections, and equipment—is a community asset, a form of commonly held social wealth. By measuring the net annual community benefits attributable to the library against its community assets (i.e., invested capital), one can calculate an annual rate of return to the community's investment in the library as a social asset.

In deciding whether to pursue only one or both of these approaches, consider first the audiences you wish to reach and the message you want to deliver. If your purpose is to advocate for greater operational funding or a local tax increase, then the first approach is adequate.

Simplest Study: Return to Annual Operating Funds

If your library is an independent political division with its own taxing authority, define costs in terms of annual locally funded operating revenues. If your library is a subdivision or department of a city, township, or county government, include all operating outlays (e.g., payroll, fringe benefits, security, maintenance, custodial, and vehicle operations, even estimates of services provided in kind by other government departments).

By comparing annual community benefits with annual local funding, cost-benefit analysis can provide a message of how much the community benefits for each dollar of annual local support—how much "bang for the buck." This analysis can produce simple, direct sound bites such as "Our library provides $2 in benefits to our community for every dollar of local tax support."

Implicit in this statement is the concept of leveraging local funds. If your library is successful in attracting federal or state funding, foundation grants, or private-sector donations, then by adding funds from these sources to local tax support the library is able to enhance services and benefits relative to each local tax dollar. This increases the local bang for the buck.

Detailed Study: Operating Returns and Rate of Return to Capital Investment

If your purpose is to advocate for a capital campaign or a bond issue, then the second approach is more appropriate. In this situation, your audiences want to know whether the library is a good investment of funds. The second approach responds to that question by quantifying the rate of return to investment in the library.

A *rate of return* is a fraction in which the numerator represents the net returns and the denominator is a measure of asset value or cost. For example, a bank certificate of deposit may pay $50 in interest for a deposit of $1,000. Thus, the rate of return is 50/1,000, or 5 percent.

For a library, the numerator measures the annual net benefits (benefits less operating costs) and the denominator measures the value of the library's capital assets, such as buildings, collections, furniture, equipment, and vehicles. Note that, because the numerator requires figures for both benefits and operating costs, calculating the rate of return requires the same figures as the first method discussed in the preceding section. If the study is to report the rate of return, the study can report benefits per dollar of operating funds as well; there is no additional research expense to do this.

Measuring the value of library assets is conceptually easy but practically difficult. We would like to know how much the library's physical assets, such as buildings, collections, furniture, equipment, and vehicles, are worth. Most libraries are not required by law, accounting conventions, or practice to maintain a balance sheet or value their assets. We address this topic in detail in chapter 6, but the general advice here is avoid appraisal methods that might understate the value of the library's assets. Undervaluing the library's assets can inflate the study's estimate of rate of return.

How large must your library's rate of return on investment be to impress audiences? Many audiences are likely to understand and appreciate comparisons of your library's CBA rate of return to returns on private-sector investments. For example, according to the *Wall Street Journal,* the average annual change in the Dow Jones Industrial Average from its inception in 1896 through 2004 is an increase of 7.6 percent.[1]

Some economists argue that the return to public-sector investment should be higher than private-sector returns to justify public-sector investment. They adjust upward for corporate income taxes on private-sector capital investment and inefficiencies caused by the tax system used to fund public investment. Even so, returns on investment of 15 percent or more should impress audiences. In our research, conservatively estimated returns to public investment in most libraries exceeded 15 percent easily.

> ASK: Is the purpose of our study to advocate for operating funds or to advocate for a capital campaign or bond issue? If for operating funds, the study should calculate benefits per dollar of local operating support. If for a capital campaign or bond issue, the study can report the rate of return to capital investment as well as benefits per dollar of local operating support.

Ensure Conservative, Defensible Results

Economists who have conducted CBA and economic impact studies are aware that consultants and their clients are often tempted to inflate the results. Don't do it. Don't overstate benefits. Don't tolerate sloppy, biased surveys that interview only the library's cheerleaders. Don't understate costs. Your reputation matters.

Professional sports teams seeking public funds for new stadiums have often released inflated economic impact studies intended to muster public support for their projects. Reporters have learned to go to academic institutions to seek unbiased appraisals of such studies. Two possible scenarios result—neither in the interest of the team that sponsored the inflated impact study. One possibility is that the newspapers run side-by-side articles reporting the team's economic impact study and the academicians' criticisms. The other is that the newspapers' headlines focus on the team's biased attempt to manipulate public sentiment through a fraudulent study, destroying the team's public relations message and undermining public trust. For your library, you want a CBA study that is credible and defensible—one that stands up to critical review and impresses the public with the library's stewardship, service, and integrity. Avoid the temptations discussed below.

Don't Overstate Benefits

When faced with choices in designing a study, choose options that understate results rather than inflate results. Always be in a position to claim and demonstrate that your library's contribution and performance meet or exceed those reported in the study.

In our experience, in most cases direct benefits are sufficient to demonstrate the library's value to the community and responsible stewardship of public resources. Measurement of indirect and non-use benefits is much more problematic and open to question (see chapter 2). All audiences understand and appreciate that a library has social impacts beyond those on individual users, but by measuring only direct benefits to users you clearly understate the total benefits to the community and increase the credibility of your study's final results.

To protect credibility and save on survey costs, use willingness to pay rather than willingness to accept for contingent valuation questions. WTP questions bring a more conservative approach to contingent valuation of benefits. An extensive literature suggests that WTA responses inflate value, which makes contingent valuation analyses based on them subject to criticism. Using both measures in one survey can confuse respondents, lengthen the survey, and increase survey costs. Restrict your contingent valuation to WTP questions.

When identifying user groups, focus on those groups that are readily identifiable and whose benefits can be credibly and validly measured by surveys at a reasonable expense. Benefits to groups that you omit are not measured in your study, which allows you to assert correctly and confidently that the benefits you do measure understate the total benefits to all users.

Similarly, when using the consumer surplus approach for individual services, don't try to measure benefits from every single, detailed service the library offers. Collapse services into categories that are relatively similar and have good private-sector analogues. Omit less significant services that are unlikely to enhance estimated value substantially. Omitting such services zeros their contribution to the library's estimated value to the community, but again this permits you to assert the conservative nature of the study's design and results. Omitting services also reduces the length of survey interviews, enhancing response rates and statistical confidence in the study's conclusions.

Don't be tempted to add measures of economic impact to inflate the size of your library's benefits unless your library is a major institution, as described in chapter 2. For all but the largest libraries, economic impact analysis is inappropriate in measurements of the benefits of a library to its community. Even if you are applying such an analysis to a state library system, you must undertake the study with care.

Don't Overstate User Counts

Valid counts of the number of active users of library services are critical to the CBA methodology outlined in this book. Libraries that cannot distinguish active from inactive cardholders, permit duplicate cardholder records in their database, or cannot filter their database for the cardholders at the same address also cannot mount a credible, defensible study. If they attempt a study, their samples of cardholders to survey contain substantial numbers of invalid or inactive cardholders. Such invalid or inactive members of the survey sample are unlikely to respond to the survey and cause response rates to plummet. Low response rates undermine statistical confidence in the study's conclusions. Although researchers can attempt to correct for such problems in their empirical estimates, the process and conclusions are likely to be suspect.

If the library cannot filter its database for members of the same household or has duplicate records for cardholders, households may receive multiple calls or invitations to participate. These households may question the study's procedures or feel that the library is unduly invasive of their privacy and inconsiderate of their family time. Furthermore, unless researchers can estimate the degree of duplication from the study's responses, the duplicate records inflate user counts and overstate the estimates of the library's benefits to the community.

Don't Tolerate Biased Survey Results

For your study to be valid, the survey results must be representative of the population of active library users. If only cardholders who use and value the library extensively respond to the surveys, the raw survey results will reflect only the very positive views of the library's biggest fans and cheerleaders. The survey results will not be representative of the population of library users. Without testing and correcting for response bias, extrapolation of survey results will overstate the total value of library benefits to all active library users and be open to challenge. Audiences or critics knowledgeable of survey methods will want assurances that your survey procedures have produced results that are representative and unbiased.

Don't Understate Costs or Value of Assets

A CBA study provides a comparison of benefits to costs. Critics can attack a study by claiming that it inflates benefits, understates costs, or both. It is just as important to avoid understating the library's costs or asset value as it is to avoid inflating estimates of the library's benefits to the community. For example, the benefit-cost ratio is a fraction that states the library's bang for the buck. Using a denominator (cost) in the fraction that is too small inflates the value of the fraction and exaggerates the library's benefits per dollar of local tax support.

Similarly, a rate of return is a fraction that depicts the library's provision of annual net benefits relative to the value of its assets. Using a denominator (assets) in the fraction that is too small inflates the value of the fraction and exaggerates the library's rate of return to the community's investment. If the library has defensible, current, comprehensive data on costs and net worth, use them. If not, select methods of estimating costs and asset value that tend to overstate rather than understate.

SUMMARY

Before commissioning a CBA study for your library, use cost-benefit reasoning to consider whether or not such a study is in your library's best interest. Consider the study's feasibility and whether the benefits the library would receive from undertaking the study outweigh the study's cost—in terms of both budget and resource commitment. Consider reasons for undertaking a CBA study.

- Is my library threatened by fiscal crisis?
- Is my library planning a capital campaign or quest for additional operating funds?
- If so, will a credible CBA study sway critical decision makers?
- Would a CBA study help me manage my library more efficiently or market library services more effectively?

Consider also reasons for not undertaking a CBA study.

- Am I confident that a CBA study will promote my library's image and role in the community and not undermine them?
- Are my library's records and staff up to the challenge of a well-executed CBA study?
- Will my budget and calendar support a well-executed CBA study?

Do the benefits of undertaking a study outweigh the costs of the study? If so, continue reading. If not, you can stop here. If you decide to proceed, begin by framing the scope of your CBA study:

- On the benefit side of the analysis, decide the level of detail with respect to services and user groups appropriate for your needs. Develop a service-user matrix depicting your choices.
- Frame the cost side of the analysis. Choose the best summary measure to meet your objectives—benefits per dollar of operating support, rate of return on investment, or both.

Finally, beware of the following pitfalls when designing and conducting your study:

- Don't overstate benefits.
- Don't overstate user counts
- Don't tolerate biased survey results.
- Don't understate costs or value of assets.

Whatever your specific audiences and objectives, your CBA study should enhance your public relations and assist you in decision making and strategic planning. Careful consideration of the study's design helps ensure that your investment in a CBA study pays off for you and your library. In the next chapters, we review in detail the steps in executing a CBA study.

NOTE

1. E. S. Browning, "A Fight to the Finish for Stocks," *Wall Street Journal,* January 3, 2006: R1.

CHAPTER 4

Preparing to Measure Benefits

ONCE YOU HAVE DECIDED TO PROCEED WITH A CBA STUDY FOR YOUR library, the next step is to lay the foundation for the study itself. This chapter offers greater detail regarding issues raised in the previous two chapters. Subjects include notifying the library board, selecting a research consultant, identifying appropriate internal staff to participate in the planning and execution of the study, constructing the service-user matrix and converting it into a survey instrument, selecting a survey agency, and establishing a budget and timeline for the execution of the study.

NOTIFYING GOVERNANCE OFFICIALS

Before seeking a research consultant and survey agency, most library directors prepare their board of directors or their department heads by presenting the library's need to conduct a CBA study. The questions from the preceding chapter should help the director prepare a preliminary presentation for the board. The focus should be on how the library can benefit from a study if the costs and time frame should prove to be acceptable to the board.

Because the final design of the study depends on the interaction of the research consultant with members of the library team, the breadth, depth, and cost of the study should be left open at this time. Most directors make a second, more detailed presentation to governing officials at a later time to get formal support for the study, its budget, and the contracts necessary to execute the study.

SELECTING AN ECONOMIST AS RESEARCH CONSULTANT

Libraries need the assistance of an economist in designing and executing CBA studies. We know of no public libraries that have an economist on staff, so you will be recruiting an economist to hire on a contractual basis for the study.

Although several economists nationally have participated in CBA studies of public libraries, you may wish to begin your search by talking with economists at local institutions of higher education. Hiring a local consultant may be less expensive than contracting one from outside your area, and a local consultant may assist you in presentations and in responding to media coverage after you complete the study. Furthermore, local academicians may have a halo of credibility with local media and audiences that consultants from outside do not, even if the outsiders have more experience performing such studies.

Start by contacting the economics department at local colleges or universities. Most schools have one or more economists on their faculty with a background in either public-sector economics (sometimes called "public finance") or environmental economics. These economists should be familiar with cost-benefit analysis and contingent valuation analysis—the core methodologies for the study.

If you wish to consider only a few local institutions, a phone call or casual conversation over lunch may be more productive than a formal request for proposals (RFP). Before that meeting, suggest that the prospective consultants might wish to look through this book to become familiar with the methodological outline you intend to follow. This book also contains technical appendixes for economists that can assist them in their research design and analysis. During your phone call or meeting, discuss the purpose and objectives of the study, tentative time frame, and role of the consultant. You also may want to discuss possible agencies to execute the surveys in the study. Many schools have survey centers, and some economists may have a working relationship with the survey center at their institution.

If you wish to solicit formal bids and proposals from several institutions, your RFP should contain the following elements:

1. Study objectives:
    a. To quantify in dollar terms a conservative estimate of the benefits provided by the public library to its community;
    b. To estimate in dollar terms the annual local fiscal support for the library, annual library operating expenses, and replacement value of library assets;
    c. To provide conservative estimates of the community's return to its investment in its public library, such as benefits per dollar of annual tax support, benefits per dollar of annual operating revenue, and benefits per dollar of library assets.

2. Approximate time frame for the study (allow at least ten months)
3. Research consultant's responsibilities:
   a. Assisting in the design of the study and adaptation of the survey instruments;
   b. Assisting in the selection of a survey agency for the study;
   c. Monitoring the survey process;
   d. Guiding and validating the collection of internal library data related to financial support, costs, and value of library assets;
   e. Estimating user benefits and summary measures of the community's return to its investment in its public library;
   f. Writing a formal report summarizing the study (for an example, see http://www.ala.org/editions/extras/Elliott09232/);
   g. Assisting the library director in presenting the study to important audiences and in responding to media inquiries.
4. Elements of a bidder's response:
   a. Name, title, institution, and contact information;
   b. Curriculum vitae or resume;
   c. Bid (ask for a fixed price for the completed project).
5. Deadline for receipt of proposals

After receiving bids, you should also interview the top candidates to ensure that you are comfortable with their interpersonal skills. Initially, the director may wish to engage the services of the research consultant on a temporary basis to help design the study, draft a grant proposal if you intend to seek external funding, select a survey agency, or construct a tentative budget. The more quickly you get your research consultant on board, the better you can facilitate the study.

Once the scope of the study, budget, and timeline are decided, the director provides this specific information to the governing officials and requests a formal expression of support. With that support, the library can engage in formal contracts with the research consultant and survey agency for the execution of the study.

IDENTIFYING LIBRARY STAFF FOR THE STUDY TEAM

Creating a small team of library staff to assist in the study design and execution is an important step to ensure the study's completion. Although the library director ultimately evaluates the study's outcomes and decides how they are to be used, the director has too many responsibilities to be the sole representative from the library's staff.

The team assists the research consultant in framing the study and acquiring necessary information from library records. It also helps the director identify important uses and audiences for the study and consider internal applications of the study's results.

The library director may wish to appoint a liaison as the director's representative to work with the research consultant and to ensure prompt and reliable execution of study tasks internal to the library. The liaison should be readily available to the research consultant. The liaison also should have the authority to make decisions regarding the study and enforce timelines to execute important steps in the study. The liaison ensures that the library addresses patron inquiries and concerns during the user surveys. The liaison also reviews drafts of the study report and conclusions and provides feedback to the research consultant. An assistant library director or assistant to the library director often can fill such a role.

The team should include representatives from the library's IT staff, finance or accounting staff, and major service divisions. The heads of the library's major service divisions assist the director, liaison, and research consultant in framing the service-user matrix. The library's IT staff validates the accuracy and completeness of the library's cardholder database, filters the database, and samples the database according to criteria provided by the research consultant. The finance or accounting staff provides information from the past year regarding the library's local financial support, operating outlays, and value of library's assets.

CONSTRUCTING THE SERVICE-USER MATRIX: A CRITICAL FIRST STEP

For a study that includes detail on benefits contributed by specific library services (see chapter 3), one of the first and most important tasks the team faces is constructing a service-user matrix to guide the detailed estimation of benefits. The service-user matrix is an array illustrating the relationship between a library's services and the patron groups that use each of those services. The research consultant should facilitate a structured brainstorming session to assist the team in developing this matrix.

Why is this matrix so important to the validity and cost of the study? First, the matrix forces the team to decide which beneficiaries of library services to include in the study. We suggested earlier, for the sake of credibility and validity, that the study survey only direct users of library services and include only their benefits in calculating the library's return to community investment. By including only benefits from direct use and avoiding the controversial measurement of indirect and non-use benefits, the study results will be more conservative, credible, and defensible.

In deciding which beneficiaries to include, the team must confront a critical trade-off. The more categories of direct user surveyed, the richer the detail regarding the distribution of benefits among client populations and the more comprehensive the measurement of benefits. The more categories of direct user surveyed, however, the greater the number of surveys that must be conducted to have confidence in the study's conclusions and, hence, the greater the cost of the surveys.

Second, the matrix forces the team to decide the level of detail with which the surveys solicit benefits derived from different library services. The more services about which detailed information is solicited, the greater the detail regarding the benefits, and the more useful the results for management of resource allocation. On the other hand, the more services about which detailed information is solicited, the longer the survey instrument, and the lower the response rate to the survey. The lower the response rate, the greater the likelihood that those who do respond are not representative of the population of library users. The greater the response bias, the less credible the survey's conclusions.

In summary, designing the service-user matrix forces the research team to balance the prospective uses and audiences for the study against the study's breadth, depth, and cost. Confronting these questions at the beginning of the research process helps to ensure that the study fulfills the library's strategic objectives at a cost the library can afford.

To initiate the design of the service-user matrix, the library director and research consultant should have the team read and reflect on the library's mission, goals, and strategic plan. What are the primary types of user the library serves? What are the major categories of service the library provides? Which constituents tend to use which categories of service?

Identify User Groups

The columns of the service-user matrix are categories of library user. Many categories of client benefit from library services. Different groups use different library services and benefit from library services in different ways. Library users can be grouped in a variety of ways:

> By those who hold active library cards versus those who do not (e.g., walk-in users)
>
> By geographic residence, such as residents of the library's taxing jurisdiction versus non-residents
>
> By the branch at which the library card was issued or by use of mobile library services
>
> By primary purpose of library use (e.g., families, educators, businesses, government agencies, not-for-profit organizations)
>
> By age (e.g., children, teens, college students, young adults, adults, seniors)
>
> By physical attributes (e.g., sight challenged, physically challenged)

How should your library group its users to measure benefits? Your team's answer to this question should reflect your library's mission. Even more important, the team's answer should reflect why your library is conducting the study and how it wishes to use the study results to achieve its strategic goals. For example, consider a public library in the county seat of a rural agricultural area. If the library's principal mission is to serve families who reside in the county and to complement the resources of the local educational institutions, then the focus of the study should be on resident households and educators in local schools. Also, if the purpose of the study is to demonstrate the library's value to the county to muster fiscal support, then presenting measures of the value of the library to resident families and the library's value as a supplement to local educational budgets will make the case persuasively. It is unlikely that broadening the scope of the study to measure benefits to walk-in users, local businesses, and not-for-profit organizations will enhance the results substantially.

Alternatively, consider the public library of a large city with several corporate headquarters and federal, state, or regional government agencies that use the library for research. The library may choose to design its study to measure separately the benefits accruing to households, education, major businesses, and government agencies— four distinct and readily identifiable categories of user. If the purpose of the study is to muster local tax support as well as grants from government, businesses, and foundations, then documenting the breadth of the library's role in the community by showing the flows of benefits to area families, educational institutions, businesses, and government agencies will make a stronger case than focusing on families and education alone.

Remember, however, that adding categories of user increases the number and complexity of the surveys of users. Make sure the value of broadening the scope of the study by adding these groups justifies the additional cost.

Identify Categories of Library Service

The rows of the service-user matrix are categories of library service. In its brainstorming session to construct the service-user matrix, the team may be tempted to categorize library services by the library's own internal organizational structure. If the library's staff is divided into departments such as administration, acquisitions, information technology, reference, fiction books, nonfiction books, periodicals, children's services, and government documents, then the team's first inclination may be to structure the measurement of library benefits around these categories. But how well will that approach serve the study's objectives?

See the Library through the Users' Eyes

Remember that the purpose of the service-user matrix is to frame the study to facilitate the measurement of benefits to library users. Only users can provide information about the benefits they receive from library services. Consequently, the categorization of library services must fit users' perceptions of services, not librarians' categories of work process. The two sets of perceptions may be similar but are not always the same. When developing the service-user matrix and survey questions, be careful to frame them in terms of how users ask for help or materials as opposed to the names or labels librarians use. The validity of the survey instrument and conclusions depends on whether users interpret correctly the questions posed to them.

Will all users, for example, understand the librarian's term "Internet access" to refer to searches or e-mail on computers? Will users interpret the librarian's term "readers' advisory" appropriately, or do most just want help finding a book or video? If asked about their reasons for using the library, some users will misconstrue the librarian's typical "research" and "reference" categories. Many might claim to be conducting "research" when simply seeking help finding information of a general (e.g., a book on the environment or "something to read" like Nora Roberts's novels) or specific (e.g., where to find a part for a rebuilt old car or the street address of a family member in 1900) nature. Also, don't let your discussion devolve into ongoing staff debates about how to organize and display collections. It needs to focus on how users ask questions and how they behave in particular user situations.

Don't Let Service Categories Overlap

The categories of service should not overlap. Ideally they should be mutually exclusive. Because the consultant eventually adds up benefits across all service categories to get total library benefits, overlap causes benefits from some services to be counted more than once and total library benefits to be overstated. For example, "Children's Services" can include children's books, audiovisual materials, and programs such as story hour. If "Books," "Audiovisual," and "Programs" are also included in the service-user matrix without any qualification, then they overlap with "Children's Services" and are likely to lead to double-counting of benefits.

Avoid Excessive Detail

Initially the team may want to create a comprehensive list of services, but again it will face a trade-off between the level of detail and the cost and validity of the study. The greater the number of categories and level of detail in the service-user matrix, the greater the number of categories and level of detail in the survey instruments. The longer the survey instruments, the higher the cost, the lower the response rate, and the lower the credibility of the study's conclusions.

Do library users benefit from the services of the administrative offices and acquisitions department? Of course, they do. But these areas of the library organization do not deliver end products or final services directly to the user; they only support that delivery. The same is true of the cataloging department. The service-user matrix should list only those categories of service that are final services or end products the users consume directly.

The team should use its judgment to winnow the categories of service and eliminate from consideration those that are not likely to contribute substantive benefit estimates. Here's an illustration: Though hard-copy reference materials such as encyclopedias and unabridged dictionaries are still important staples of many libraries' reference collections, our CBA research shows that few households value these enough to consider buying them on their own. And when they do buy reference materials, they tend to buy inexpensive paperbacks or software, not a relatively expensive hardbound set of encyclopedias. Hence, the estimated dollar benefits they associate with such materials (other than special collections) are likely to be small. A better strategy might be to measure benefits associated with access to electronic reference databases (including both those compiled locally and those from commercial publishers) rather than to seek detail on use of bound general reference materials. Similarly, though having a collection of large-print or braille materials may be important in serving the sight-challenged population, listing such categories separately in the service-user matrix invites overlap with other categories and also adds little to the estimated dollar value of total benefits. Look back at table 2.2 for the service categories used in our studies of medium-sized and smaller public libraries.

Draft Survey Instruments from the Service-User Matrix

Each column in the service-user matrix represents a separate population of library users (a niche market for library services). The research consultant and library liaison must develop a strategy to sample each of these user populations. The research consultant must draft a survey instrument to solicit that population's service benefits. Our own survey instruments for households and educators and for businesses can serve as a starting point in drafting the survey instruments (see appendix C).

Each cell in the service-user matrix becomes a block of questions in a survey instrument. To shorten the length of actual interviews, our computer-assisted telephone interviews and Web-based instruments use a filtering question early in the interview. The filtering question asks the respondent to select from a list of services only those services the household uses. The survey instrument then branches only to those blocks of questions corresponding to the service categories the respondent selects. Respondents are never asked any detail about service categories they do not use. Because the literature on surveys suggests that the order of questions influences responses, the computerized survey instruments randomize the order in which the interviewers ask about categories of service the respondent selects.

Design a Survey Strategy

Before contacting survey agencies as possible partners for the study, the consultant and director should agree on a tentative survey strategy to propose to the survey agencies. Consider separately each of the user populations identified in the service-user matrix. What is the best way of contacting each of these populations to obtain a statistically valid set of responses?

We have found that executing the household (general user) surveys in two waves—a Web-based survey backed by telephone interviews—results in an exceptional response rate at a reasonable cost. At one of our IMLS research sites for medium-sized libraries, we requested that the director invite a random sample of cardholding households to access and complete a Web-based survey. This request resulted in a response rate exceeding 20 percent among households in this upper-middle-class, computer-literate library service area. Follow-up telephone interviews with those not responding by Web doubled the final response rate to 45 percent. The only statistically significant response bias detected in this research was a disproportionately higher response rate from households with adult cardholders as opposed to households where the only cardholders were youths.

This particular library had current and accurate records in their cardholder database and a talented IT staff, so the original sample had few bad records (inactive cards, invalid mailing addresses, incomplete or wrong phone numbers, etc.). A sample of 2,500 cardholder records yielded almost 1,000 usable, completed survey responses and interviews—approximately 40 percent. Most researchers hope to see response rates of at least 25 percent with 600 usable, completed interviews. Conservatively then, to obtain 600 valid responses, the original sample size would have to have between 1,500 (i.e., 600/0.4) and 2,400 (i.e., 600/0.25) households.

To survey educators, we have found that asking responding households to self-identify library-using educators in the households yields good results at negligible additional cost. In this strategy, at the end of the household interview, self-identified educators answer additional questions focused on their professional use of the library.

Large urban libraries that have special programs for specific client schools may, however, wish to perform separate surveys of educators at those schools. The sampling strategy for such a survey should be tailored to the study for that particular library. In many cases, because the number of educators associated with the client schools is likely to be relatively small, the library attempts to get answers from the entire population of educators served by these special services rather than use a sample survey. A survey of an entire population is termed a *census*. The number of completions in such a census need not be 600 or higher for statistical validity. Instead, the study should seek a high response rate, and the research consultant will use small-sample statistical analysis to draw inferences about the corresponding user population.

Similarly, a large library that offers special services or collections to other distinctive user groups such as businesses, government agencies, or nonprofit organizations may wish to conduct separate surveys targeting each of those user groups. The sampling strategies for such surveys should be tailored to the study for that particular library. In many cases, such surveys are censuses of each of the unique populations served by these special services. Each of the survey instruments should be customized for the services unique to its specific user group.

In summary, before the research consultant or library liaison can solicit or negotiate with a survey agency, the team must decide the breadth and depth of the study and its surveys:

> *How many different user populations* must be sampled and interviewed?
> *How many interviews must be completed from each population* to ensure statistical confidence in population estimates from the sample?
>
> *What is the expected length in minutes* of an average interview for each of the user populations to be surveyed?
>
> *What strategies* might be used to survey each of the target populations of library users?

Having developed tentative answers to these questions, the director and consultant are ready to approach potential partner survey agencies.

SELECTING A SURVEY AGENCY

Many libraries already have or have had relationships with survey agencies. If yours does not, the research consultant or library liaison can identify university survey centers and private survey firms from which to solicit bids for the study surveys.

Criteria

Essential characteristics to evaluate in selecting a survey agency include the following:

1. *Professionalism of the agency's personnel.*
   a. The reliability of the study depends on the quality and accuracy of the survey data. It is imperative that the survey agency preserve the integrity of the statistical sampling and the research process. Be sure that the survey agency has experience in scientific sample surveys and a reputation for integrity.
   b. Interviewers must be courteous and considerate. The respondents to the survey are your library's patrons. Telephone interviewers are calling on behalf of the library director and must be good ambassadors

for the library without biasing responses to survey questions. A CBA study should enhance public relations with your library's patrons, not undermine them. When approached properly, many patrons are flattered that the library is seeking their perspective. Furthermore, courteous, considerate interviewers enhance survey response rates and thus the credibility of the study.

2. *Experience in conducting both Web-based surveys and computer-assisted telephone interviews.* We suggest using Web-based surveys backed by telephone interviews to achieve the highest response rates at the lowest cost. The survey agency should have the capability of conducting both Web-based and computer-assisted follow-up telephone surveys.

3. *The ability to provide the Web-based and telephone survey responses in a file format acceptable to the research consultant.*

4. *Timeliness.* The survey agency must have the ability to execute surveys and deliver survey results in a time frame consistent with the study timeline.

5. *Cost.* The cost of the study and surveys depends on the number of user groups about which you want separate information and the length of the survey instruments. The cost can also vary with the timeline you set for the study.

Academic versus Private Survey Agencies

University survey centers and private agencies often have different strengths and weaknesses in conducting surveys. The strengths of the university survey centers tend to lie in the areas of cost, credibility, and response rates:

Public universities have a public service mission, which may permit them to offer services to a public library at a reduced rate. If the research consultant is an academician, the researcher may have a relationship with a university survey center. This relationship may facilitate execution of the surveys and perhaps result in a discount for survey costs.

In a Web-based survey, respondents may be more likely to trust a university survey center to respect their privacy and right to confidentiality.

Respondents may also be more willing to accept telephone calls from a university research center than from a private survey firm.

Audiences to which the library eventually presents the study results may view university survey centers as more objective and therefore give greater credence to the study's conclusions.

On the other hand, the weaknesses of university survey centers are in the area of experience of interviewers and flexibility of scheduling:

> University survey centers often use less-experienced student interviewers, whereas some private firms may employ more mature, experienced interviewers who have worked at the interview firm for a relatively long time.

> University survey centers may be less flexible in scheduling interviews and surveys than private firms.

Under the purview of the research consultant, the library samples each of the user populations and provides the contact lists for each sample of user groups. The survey agency should not construct the contact lists. Procedures for sampling the library's databases to develop the contact lists are outlined in chapter 5.

ESTIMATING THE BUDGET

Before returning to governing officials to solicit their formal support for a study, the director and consultant collaborate in estimating a tentative budget for completing the study. The following budget itemizes only out-of-pocket expenses for the library and does not include commitments of personnel and resources internal to the library:

1. Contract for the research consultant
2. Contract for the survey agency
3. Copying (or printing) and postage for letters from the library director to samples of library users inviting them to respond to the surveys
4. Marketing and media materials for the study's conclusion (gifts for participants, travel if for a large library district, stationery and envelopes for initial survey letter and then a thank-you letter)

ESTABLISHING A TIMELINE
FOR THE STUDY

How long will the study take? Table 4.1 outlines the major steps in executing a study, suggests the approximate time to allocate to each step, and assigns responsibility for the associated tasks. A CBA study can be completed in ten to twelve months if the library adopts the methodology presented here and adapts the included survey instruments.

TABLE 4.1
Estimated timeline

TIME ELAPSED	TIME REQUIRED	ACTIVITY	RESPONSIBILITY
Two months	Two months	Identify and recruit research consultant.	Director
		Identify library team and liaison.	Director
		Construct service-user matrix. Reach consensus on breadth and depth of benefit surveys.	Consultant and library team
		Develop overview, tentative budget, and timeline for study.	Consultant and director
		Obtain formal board support for study.	Director
		Contract with research consultant and survey agency.	Director
Three months	One month	Adapt and refine survey instruments (allow for more time if developing your own instruments).	Consultant
		Test databases by pulling sample records.	Consultant and IT department
Five months	Two months	Program Web-based and CATI instruments.	Survey agency
		Train interviewers for telephone survey.	Consultant and survey agency
		Field-test instruments.	Consultant and survey agency
		Prepare draft of invitational letters.	Library liaison
		Pull random samples of cardholder databases.	Consultant and IT department
		Inform library staff and establish procedures to answer patron questions about the surveys and study.	Director and liaison
		Prepare labels, letterhead, and envelopes.	Library liaison
		Advertise or inform community of survey.	Library liaison
		Mail invitational letters.	Library liaison
Eight months	Three months	Execute survey in the field.	Survey agency
		Produce income statements.	Library liaison
		Produce valuation of assets.	Library liaison
Ten months	Two months	Analyze data.	Consultant
		Prepare response rate and preliminary data.	Consultant
		Prepare draft of executive summary and report.	Consultant
		Review and revise executive summary and report.	Liaison and consultant
		Prepare media releases and publicity.	Liaison and consultant
		Present results to target audiences.	Director and consultant

SUMMARY

Initiation of a CBA study rests on the shoulders of the library director. Having evaluated the need for the study as in chapter 3, the director may wish to inform governance officials that the library will explore the feasibility of a CBA study. Next the director should identify possible economists in the area, especially those associated with local colleges, to serve as a research consultant for the study. The consultant can assist the director and the director's internal team in designing the study by facilitating their construction of a service-user matrix for the library. Based on the service-user matrix, the consultant and director can outline the study and evaluate prospective survey agencies. Having selected a survey agency, the consultant and director can prepare an outline, budget, and timeline for the study to present to governing officials for their formal approval and support.

CHAPTER 5

Measuring Library Benefits
Identifying and Sampling Library Users

THE MOST DIFFICULT, CRITICAL, AND COSTLY STEP OF YOUR CBA study is the execution of surveys to determine the benefits library users receive from library services. Although many of the tasks outlined in this chapter and the next fall to the research consultant and survey agency, it is important that the library director and library's liaison understand how measurement is accomplished and are prepared to assign and manage the critical library staff participation in the measurements. This chapter and chapter 6 on measuring benefits present each of these steps in detail.

CRITICAL STEPS AND ROLES

The critical steps and roles in measuring benefits include the following:

> The consultant, with guidance from the project liaison and the library's IT staff, designs a plan for random sampling of the library's user databases.

> The consultant, working with the liaison and conferring with selected library staff, tailors survey instruments to the library under study.

> Library staff members, under the supervision of the liaison, execute the sampling plan to provide lists of potential respondents and their contact information.

> The library staff, under supervision of the liaison, mails an invitation from the library director inviting selected library patrons to participate in the surveys.

The survey agency, subject to oversight by the research consultant, programs and field-tests the survey instruments.

After the survey agency has completed the surveys and delivered the data files, the consultant analyzes the survey responses and estimates benefits to the library's service area.

Following up on the survey work, the library staff, under the supervision of the liaison, acknowledges the library users who participated in the surveys and expresses the library's appreciation.

FOLLOW FEDERAL GUIDELINES TO PROTECT YOUR LIBRARY USERS

Before reviewing the detailed procedures below, take special note of how to protect respondents' identities and confidential answers to your surveys. Our best advice is to obey the law, specifically the federal government's Guidelines for the Conduct of Research Involving Human Subjects.[1] Research universities that accept federal grants already adhere to this law. University policies addressing these guidelines typically require prior review and approval by an internal committee of research faculty. Before the study can begin, the committee, comparing the proposed research plan against the guidelines, reviews and approves the plan's procedures, instruments, and protocol for record keeping.

A CBA study of the type outlined in this book holds little risk for those who provide survey answers. Following the federal guidelines, however, provides appropriate (and legal) answers to questions someone might raise about how you are protecting the privacy of your users. The library and its partners in the study should take care to follow the policies and procedures as required and to build any such approval processes into their research and communication timeline.

SCHEDULING THE SURVEYS

Consider carefully the calendar for your surveys. Surveys of general users are likely to have the highest response rates in late winter and early spring. Avoid summer vacations when many library users are not easy to contact. Avoid the tumult in fall when some families are coping with sending children back to school and others are engaged in harvesttime, sending whole families of seasonal workers into the fields. Also avoid hassling library users with surveys during the hectic winter holidays. For businesses, avoid popular vacation times, major reorganizations of large firms, and the close of the fiscal year.

SAMPLING THE LIBRARY'S DATABASES OF USERS

The service-user matrix and survey strategies discussed in chapter 4 can guide a consultant in developing sampling plans for the library's databases of users. Each column in the service-user matrix corresponds to a particular user group from which the library seeks detailed information regarding usage and benefits. A consultant can begin by asking what records the library has about individual users in each of the user group categories identified in the matrix.

General Users (Households)

Defining "General User" for Sampling and Surveys

For most smaller and medium-sized libraries and many larger libraries, a CBA study surveys only one population—general users. "General users" are defined here as *active* cardholding households, specifically cardholders who have completed a statistically recorded transaction, whether virtual or at a library facility, during the previous twelve months. A cardholding household consists of one or more library cardholders who list the same postal address in their library record. In other words, you should include no more than one cardholder from each household—no matter how many adult or juvenile cardholders reside in that household.

Note that the goal here is to sample active cardholding *households*, not active individual cardholders. This distinction is important for several reasons.

First, to protect the privacy and safety of the library's cardholding youth, the library should invite only adults to answer the Web survey or to respond to the telephone survey. Most parents do not want their children to visit websites that request personal information or to respond to telephone calls by a survey agency, especially without adult supervision. Furthermore, the library should not encourage such activities by legally defined children.

Second, the purpose of the survey is to estimate benefits from library services in dollars by asking economic decision makers about their willingness to make household purchases that would replace library services. In most states, persons under the legal age of adulthood—generally eighteen—may not make a contract. This age limit on contract making guided us in determining who could answer a household survey about all library users. We, of course, are aware that many youth exercise discretion and even control over a good deal of household spending, but we believe the totality of spending that might substitute for library use is better addressed by a family adult with more control over the total household budget. Responses by an adult who is involved in the financial decisions of the household and has some knowledge of the household's patterns of library use, therefore, are deemed more valid than responses from a child.

Third, in many households, several members of the household may use others' library cards, including adults using their children's cards. Combining the responses for a household is likely to capture a more comprehensive and accurate picture of the household's library use and value of benefits than considering only use by the cardholder(s), especially if only children in the household possess library cards.

Fourth, we seek responses that include on-site usage, such as librarians' assistance with a reference question or homework assignment, or reading for fun without checking out a book or magazine. Many family library uses do not involve computer transactions. We believe that parents and guardians are more capable of assessing comprehensively the value of household members' library use, including nontransactional use, than are children. The comments and anecdotes supplied by those surveyed in our studies of fourteen different libraries reflected this kind of use not recorded in computerized transactions.

Using the Library's Cardholder Records to Design the Sampling Procedure

The starting point for the sampling procedure is the library's cardholder database. The consultant should meet with the liaison and a representative of the library's IT staff to learn about the library's cardholder database and its maintenance. Begin by reviewing the fields and format for a cardholder's record in the database. Helpful questions include the following:

1. Does the library purge the computerized records of inactive library users from its database?
   a. If so, what criteria are applied?
   b. How often does the library purge inactive records from its database?
   c. Does the current computer record reflect the last date of use?
2. What is the format for the address field?
   a. How is it coded?
   b. Is the coding consistent and standardized across all records?
   c. How often is the address field validated or maintained?
   d. Can the library's IT staff use the address field to match records (i.e., cardholders) that have the same address?
3. What is the format of the field for the cardholder's telephone number?
   a. Is it required?
   b. Is the coding consistent and standardized across all records?
   c. How often is the telephone number validated or maintained?

d. Can the library's IT staff use the telephone field to match records (i.e., cardholders) that share the same number?

4. Does the record contain a valid e-mail address for the cardholder?

   a. Does the library require an e-mail address in a cardholder's record?

   b. Is the coding consistent and standardized across all records?

5. Does the record include a birth date?

   a. Or, does the record distinguish between an adult cardholder and a teen or child?

   b. How?

6. Does the record identify types of cardholder that should be excluded from the survey, such as library staff and board members? Including such cardholders in the survey might cause observers to question the objectivity of benefit estimates from the study.

7. Does the record distinguish between residents and non-residents of the library's local taxing jurisdiction?

   a. If so, does the library wish to measure benefits to residents only?

   b. Or, does the library wish to measure residents' benefits separately from benefits to non-residents?

8. What information in the user record might serve as a check on response bias?

   a. For example, does the record reflect intensity of use over the previous year in terms of number of transactions or frequency of transactions?

   b. Does the record reflect when a card was first issued to the user?

Based on answers to the questions above, the consultant and liaison prescribe criteria that the library's IT staff uses to write a sampling program. The program draws random samples of library cardholders who will receive invitations from the library director to participate in the surveys.

We are emphatic that your research team should pursue this list of exploratory questions because we encountered numerous problems with cardholder databases in our CBA studies of libraries. Library directors often were shocked by the number and types of errors the study revealed in their databases. If your library cardholder database is riddled with errors, then it cannot produce an accurate count or reliable samples of users for a CBA study, much less a base on which you can do accurate service planning. Hence, in preparing for your CBA study, approach your own library's database with fresh eyes and skepticism as to the quality of the data recorded there.

The first step is to reduce the library's database of card records to a database that contains only records of active, cardholding households. Question 1 is critical to this step. Before sampling the database, IT staff must filter the database on the basis of whether cardholders are active or inactive. Why? One of the objectives of the study is to determine the value of benefits from direct use of library services *during the past year.* Those cardholders who have not used the library during the past year are considered inactive for the purpose of measuring benefits and should not participate in the survey. The IT staff should include in their sampling program statements that eliminate from further consideration those cardholder records that show no use during the past year.

Questions 2 and 3 explore the feasibility of reducing the library's cardholder database from a population of individual cardholders to a population of cardholding households. Eliminating duplication is important to avoid sampling more than one cardholder record from each household. If more than one cardholder from a household is included in the sample, then the household will receive multiple letters and calls regarding the survey. Many households find duplicate contacts annoying, and duplication reduces the credibility of the survey process.

Eliminating duplication is also important to the accuracy of counting the number of active cardholding households that used the library during the past year. After completion of the surveys, this count is necessary for the consultant's accurate estimation of total benefits to the whole cardholding population from the benefits reported by the sample interviewees. If records with the same addresses or phone numbers are retained in the database, then the count of households will be too high and cause the consultant to overestimate total library benefits.

The consultant and IT staff should decide how to filter the records in the library's active cardholder database so that the resulting database represents only active library-using households. They may choose one or both of two strategies:

> Identify cardholder records that have the same mailing address. Then retain only one record for each address.

> Identify cardholder records that have the same telephone number. Then retain only one record for each telephone number.

> Combine the first two methods. Identify cardholder records that have either the same mailing address or the same telephone number. Then retain only one record for each set of records sharing an address or a telephone number.

We prefer the third strategy because it is the most conservative of the three and minimizes duplication of contacts during the survey stage of the study.

The IT staff's sampling program should retain only records that contain a valid address and either a valid phone number or a valid e-mail address (see question 4). The sampling program should contain a filter that culls records with an incomplete address and flags records with an incomplete phone field or incomplete e-mail address.

There are many reasons for eliminating incomplete or invalid cardholder records. First, the library must have some way of contacting cardholders to invite them to participate in the survey. If the mailing address is not valid and the cardholder has no e-mail address, the library cannot send the cardholder an invitation to participate in the survey. Furthermore, if the phone number is not valid, the survey agency cannot follow up by telephone if the household does not respond to the Web survey. Finally, if the address or phone number is not complete, the record cannot be matched successfully against others to avoid duplication. Duplication inflates the count of active households and results in overstated estimates of library benefits to the community.

Question 5 is important to distinguish adult cardholders from cardholding teens or young children. If the cardholder database contains a record for an adult at a particular address or phone number, then the IT staff's program should retain only one adult card for each household and cull any other adult or youth cards associated with that address or phone number. If no adult card exists for a particular address or phone number, then the program should retain only one teen's or child's record in the database that is to be used for sampling. All correspondence or interviews are directed to the parent or guardian of a juvenile cardholder.

Question 6 addresses concerns regarding cardholders whose responses to survey questions might be biased or whose inclusion in the samples would raise questions about the objectivity of the study. Clearly library staff and board members are self-interested parties. It is prudent and conservative to exclude their households from the sampling so that they do not participate in the surveys. The program should, however, count their households in the population of active cardholding households.

Question 7 can provide useful information if the library's objective is to measure benefits only to resident households that support the library through local taxes or households that might vote in local elections and referenda. In deciding whether or not to include non-resident households in the survey, consider whether the audiences for the study's results are likely to view substantial benefits to non-residents positively or negatively.

For example, if your library has reciprocal agreements with other jurisdictions that permit residents to obtain library cards in neighboring jurisdictions, then measuring benefits to both residents and non-residents would probably be viewed positively. In such a case, keep both resident and non-resident households in the sample and consider stratifying the sample on this characteristic of the record. Stratification is explained in the next section of this chapter.

On the other hand, especially if there is no system of reciprocity between your library and others, some audiences might view services to non-residents negatively, as free riders. They may perceive non-residents' use as tying up materials residents might wish to access while paying little or nothing to support the library. If so, then consider culling the records of non-resident households from the cardholder database and population counts before sampling.

Question 8 explores information in the cardholder database that can be used to stratify the database for sampling, test for survey response bias in the survey results, or correct for response bias in the survey results.

Stratifying the Sample of Households

Statisticians use *stratification* to ensure that a sample is representative of the population from which it is drawn. In a library CBA study, the relevant population is the database of active library-using households described in the preceding section. In other words, the purpose of stratification is to ensure that the sample has the same composition as the population of active library-using households with respect to certain critical characteristics of its members.

For example, assume that the library wishes to survey both resident and non-resident cardholders but wishes to compare benefit estimates for the two sets of households. Suppose that the library's IT staff reports 11,000 active cardholding households in the library's cardholder database. A validation check of a small sample of records suggests, however, that 10 percent of the records may be invalid because of previously undiscovered data errors or coding errors; thus, at least 90 percent of the records appear to be valid. The IT staff now sorts the database of active cardholding households into separate subpopulations of resident households and non-resident households. Of the 11,000 active cardholding households, 80 percent are resident households (8,800 resident households) and 20 percent are non-resident households (2,200 non-resident households).

Based on the library's past response rates to surveys or on the response rates suggested in this book, the consultant assumes a conservative response rate for the survey—say, 25 percent. Since 90 percent of the records are expected to be valid, the expected number of net valid completed responses to the survey is 25 percent of 90 percent of the records in a sample. The sample size necessary to obtain 600 valid completed survey responses is thus $600/(0.25 \times 0.9)$, or about 2,667 records, and the sampling fraction is 2,667/11,000, or 24.24 percent. This means that the IT staff, using random sampling, should select 2,133 resident records ($8,800 \times 0.2424$) and 533 non-resident records ($2,200 \times 0.2424$), yielding a total sample of 2,666 records for the library to invite to participate in the survey.

The example above illustrates only one dimension of stratification a library might wish to consider. If the study uses a Web survey, are those cardholders with an e-mail address more likely to respond than others? If so, responses may reflect an age or income bias that requires the consultant to apply a corrective weighting to the final results. Hence, the consultant could stratify the sample by using presence or absence of an e-mail address in the record.

Our research suggests that those who use the library more frequently or intensively are more likely to respond to a survey. If so, then the survey will have a response bias and will overstate the benefit estimates (unless the consultant corrects for the bias). In other words, if the survey respondents tend to be the library's biggest fans, then the benefits that they report will be larger than if a truly random sample of library users had responded. Estimates of total library benefits based on sample responses dominated by the library's most enthusiastic cheerleaders will be too high.

The consultant can anticipate this bias and guard against it. First, the consultant can stratify the sample based on recorded library usage, ensuring that the sample of users the library contacts is representative of the spectrum of library users. Then, once the survey is completed, the consultant can check the usage records of those responding versus the original stratification. If the statistical test (typically a chi-square contingency test) rejects the hypothesis that the responding households are distributed similarly to the original sample with respect to use, then the consultant can weight the sample responses to reflect the original stratification and correct for the response bias. Estimates of benefits based on the weighted sample responses are less likely to be biased (see appendix D).

If the library has a comprehensive and well-maintained cardholder database, the consultant and liaison have many possible stratifying variables from which to choose. In making decisions about which stratifying variables to employ in the sampling procedures and in what degree of detail, they face a trade-off. The greater the number of stratifying criteria selected, the greater the number of subpopulations to sample.

Stratification can improve the accuracy of the sampling and surveys, but stratification that is too complex or detailed can create other problems. If the stratification is too complex, it complicates IT's programming to produce the samples. The more complex the programming, the greater the time required and the greater the chance for programming errors. Complex stratification can also raise the question of whether some small subpopulations require oversampling to ensure adequate representation.

To address this trade-off between accuracy and complexity, pick only those stratifying variables that address a specific objective of the study (e.g., distinguishing between benefits to residents and non-residents). Also, pick stratifying variables that help guard against and correct for response bias (e.g., frequency or intensity of library use). Besides residency and intensity of use, consider stratifying according to whether the household has adult cardholders or only youth cardholders. Also consider stratification by residence clustered by ZIP code or library branch (especially if residential patterns are correlated with the socioeconomic status or ethnicity of households).

Once the consultant and liaison have agreed on a tentative stratification strategy, IT should run a cross-tabulation to count the number of active cardholding households in each of the subpopulations identified by the stratification. If the number of households in certain cells is small, consider collapsing the design by merging some of the cells (see table 5.1 for an example). Once the stratification is completed, the IT staff can draw a subsample from each of the subpopulations. Together, these subsamples constitute the sample of active cardholders the library invites to participate in the survey.

TABLE 5.1

Cross-tabulation of stratification

	RESIDENT	NON-RESIDENT	TOTAL
Cross-tabulation of cardholding households using stratification by residency and intensity of use			
Heavy user (>60 transactions)	880	220	1,100
Moderate user (30–60 transactions)	6,160	1,540	7,700
Light user (<30 transactions)	1,760	440	2,200
Total	8,800	2,200	11,000
Applying a sampling fraction of 24.24%			
Heavy user (>60 transactions)	213	53	267
Moderate user (30–60 transactions)	1,493	373	1,866
Light user (<30 transactions)	427	107	533
Total	2,133	533	2,666
Expected responses if no bias			
Heavy user (>60 transactions)	48	12	60
Moderate user (30–60 transactions)	336	84	420
Light user (<30 transactions)	96	24	120
Total	480	120	600

Note that at least two non-resident cells are rather small (12, 24). If the critical concerns are to compare benefits of resident and non-resident cardholders while avoiding response bias among residents due to intensity of use, then collapse the design by consolidating the non-resident cardholders:

		TOTAL
Non-resident cardholders		120
Resident cardholders		480
Heavy user (>60 transactions)	48	
Moderate user (30–60 transactions)	336	
Light user (<30 transactions)	96	
Total		600

The ultimate response rate for non-resident cardholders may be less than 25 percent. If so, the number of non-resident responses may be less than 120, and the number of heavy and light non-resident users responding would be even smaller than 12 and 24. Sampling non-resident users as one subpopulation probably will not compromise the integrity of the research. If the consultant does have concerns about bias, then consider oversampling heavy and light non-resident subpopulations.

Random Sampling

Once the database of active cardholding households is sorted into subpopulations according to strata and there is a count for each subpopulation, the next step is to apply random sampling. After talking with the survey agency, the consultant and liaison can instruct the library's IT staff to follow one of two sampling protocols.

The first and simpler method is to apply the sampling fraction to each of the subpopulations. This is the method portrayed in table 5.1. If the data can be exported into a statistical software package, executing the sampling should be easy. If not, the IT staff can write its own program.

For example, if the cross-tabulation calls for 213 resident heavy users out of a subpopulation totaling 880 (see the upper-right cells in table 5.1), then the IT program should sample that subpopulation 213 times (without replacement). In its first iteration, the program generates a random number between 1 and 880. The random number represents the position of a record in the database for that subpopulation. If, for example, the first random number drawn is 183, then the program extracts the 183rd record in the database as the first record in the subsample of resident cardholding households who have recorded more than sixty transactions during the past year. There are now 879 records remaining in the subpopulation, and from them a second random number is generated—say, 562—so the 562nd record is extracted for the sample. This process is repeated until 213 records are selected. Then the whole procedure is reapplied to the next subpopulation until samples have been selected for all subpopulations of interest.

Though it is simple, this sampling protocol does have a disadvantage. The survey agency must make serious attempts to complete interviews with all cardholders whose records are included in the sample, even if this procedure should result in more than the predetermined goal of 600 completed interviews.

For example, of the 2,666 households in the sample, suppose that 300 households respond by Web. The survey agency should attempt to contact the 2,366 remaining households by telephone and complete as many interviews as possible. The survey agency should *not* merely start calling non-respondents and stop when it reaches 300 completed telephone interviews, for a total 600 Web and telephone completions. The order of the household records in the database is not likely to be random. If the records in the sample are sorted by strata, for example, just calling in order until reaching the desired number of completions may seriously bias the response.

Because most consultants use a conservative estimate of the response rate in determining the sample size, this process of calling the whole sample can result in more completions than necessary and a higher bill from a survey agency if the contract calls for the agency to be paid according to the number of completions. Furthermore, if the survey agency uses the whole sample to reach 600 records, the actual response rate will be *at best* the response rate used by the consultant to estimate the sample size.

The second and alternative process requires more complex programming to draw the sample but saves on survey time, effort, and expense. In this procedure, the sample of 2,666 households is selected as a set of stratified subsamples, each representative of the population. For example, IT could write a program to select 26 subsamples of 100 records each. Each subsample of 100 should have proportionate representation across the strata; in this example, each subsample should consist of 80 resident and 20 non-resident households. Then, if 300 of the 2,666 respond by Web, the survey agency can begin with the first sample of 100 and try to add as many telephone completions as possible to the Web responses from that subsample, then move to the second subsample of 100, and so on until 600 Web and telephone completions have been obtained. If executed earnestly, this approach maximizes survey response rate and minimizes the cost of surveys billed on the basis of number of completed interviews.

Appendix B illustrates instructions to the library's IT staff. The instructions review the issues of valid address and phone fields, reducing the cardholder database to active cardholding households, sample stratification, and random sampling.

Other Library Users

Educators

Most libraries are essential partners of local preschool and K–12 public and private schools. Moreover, many libraries offer advice, resources, and materials to support parents who are homeschooling their children. Some public libraries also complement academic libraries at area colleges in supporting student and faculty study and scholarship. Because support of local educational programs and institutions is such an important and valued part of their mission, most public libraries include educators as a separate user group in their service-user matrix.

Some large libraries offer special services to local educational institutions. If your library does this, then the librarians responsible for these special services probably maintain a list of contacts. The library can use its contact list to evaluate the benefits associated with these services. The consultant and liaison should tailor a survey instrument to the specific services offered. If desired, the survey agency may contact as many of its educational clients as it can reach rather than use a random sample to measure the extent of their usage.

If the library has no separate database of educators or educational institutions with which it has a special relationship, then the evaluation of benefits from support of local educational programs can piggyback on the survey of households, as described in chapter 4. The household survey invites respondents to self-identify educators in the household who use the library in support of their profession. By Web or by telephone, these educators then answer a separate set of questions appended to the household survey.

Businesses, Investors, Not-for-Profits, and Government Agencies

Larger libraries often have a section or special set of services focused on local businesses and investors. If the library has a client list or a special registration system for using these services, then it can use these lists to evaluate the benefits associated with these services. The consultant and liaison should tailor a survey instrument to the specific services offered. The library may want the survey agency to contact as many of its business and investor clients as it can rather than take a random sampling of them.

Alternatively, it is important to recognize that some business professionals and investors may not be identified on such lists, or they may use library services that are not housed in the business section of the library. They may use periodicals and newspapers, maps, government documents, audiovisual materials, and even the Internet in support of their activities and interests. Most will have active library cards and be eligible for the household survey. Thus, the household survey can explore benefits to these users if they are identified at the outset as a user group of interest and the household instrument includes survey questions addressing their business uses.

Not-for-profits and government agencies are often such a small part of the user population that they are not worth the cost of sampling separately. Only the largest urban libraries should consider surveying such users separately. For example, the Free Library of Philadelphia houses the Regional Foundation Center, a special section of the library serving not-for-profit agencies, foundations, grant agencies, and consultants. The Free Library's Regional Foundation Center is affiliated with the Foundation Center, headquartered in New York City.[2] The library provides materials, database subscriptions, assistance, and training regarding sources of funding, grant writing, and networking. The librarian who supervises this area has a list of contacts and clients the library could invite to respond to a survey to evaluate these services.

Unrecorded Use: Walk-in Users

Through the many presentations we have made about our CBA research, we have heard concerns that our methodology does not value walk-in use by non-cardholders. In some libraries, a few staff members have even claimed that walk-in or telephone use constitutes most of the demand for certain library services. Reference is the most frequent "special use" librarians identify as taking a lot of staff time. Further, staff members assert that reference must create a high amount of value because the users' questions are so complex.

We have carefully considered including measurement of value to walk-in users whose service may not generate a cardholder transaction. To ensure transportability, the CBA methodology we outline in this book is built on statistical and accounting practices that are used in practically all libraries. These practices include records for costs of materials, staff, and buildings along with records for circulation, virtual reserves, and other transactions. We recognize, of course, that statistical methodologies for counting in-library use already exist as well. In addition, both commercial and in-house survey instruments for measuring and checking user satisfaction about that use already exist. We could adapt such methodologies to assess the primary benefits associated with these uses. We do not advocate adding these components to those outlined in this volume, however, because to do so would add substantially to the cost of a CBA study.

Neither our research team nor the officials we worked with in our fourteen library studies believe that adding such components would contribute much value beyond what our methodology captures far more easily. As one director noted, most of the walk-in users he saw visiting his libraries were persons who already had library cards. In general, they tended to be satisfied repeat customers who came to the library when they had some question they were confident that the library staff—or a particular set of materials or a specialized database—would address.

In summary, we do not advocate including special surveys to capture value to walk-in users. The incremental benefits measured are not likely to be worth the added research expense. Excluding specific benefits to walk-in users merely makes any estimate of library value more conservative.

SUMMARY

The most difficult, critical, and costly step of your CBA study is the execution of surveys. The library director and library's liaison must understand the design and execution of the sample of library users and be prepared to assign and manage library staff who help in this process. The critical steps in this process include

- designing a plan for random sampling of the library's user databases
- drafting the survey instruments
- executing the sampling plan to extract lists of potential respondents and their contact information
- inviting selected library patrons to participate in the surveys
- field-testing the survey instruments
- analyzing the survey responses and estimates of benefits to the library's service area
- thanking the library users who participated in the surveys

This chapter addresses how to identify and sample groups of active library users. The library, its consultant, and survey agency all must adhere to strict guidelines to protect the privacy of library users who participate in the surveys. The timeline for the study should ensure that the surveys are in the field during times likely to maximize survey response rates.

By surveying only households that are active users of your library services, your library can minimize survey expense and harassment of your patrons. Filter the library's cardholder database to retain only records used during the previous twelve months. Filter out records with incomplete addresses and then reduce the database to only one record per address. Design a sampling plan to extract a random sample of general users from the filtered database.

For reliable results, the sampling plan must guard against response bias. For a survey of general users, the use of stratified random sampling promotes outcomes that are representative but also provides opportunities to check results for bias in case they are not. For educators, businesses, or other important user groups, the research design may call for censuses rather than samples. Surveys of walk-in users may not add substantially to the study results.

Now that we have identified library users who can provide us with essential information about library benefits, how do we ask them about this information? The next chapter addresses the design of survey instruments to measure benefits from library services.

NOTES

1. National Institutes of Health, *Guidelines for the Conduct of Research Involving Human Subjects*, available at http://ohsr.od.nih.gov/guidelines/graybook.html.
2. See http://www.library.phila.gov/rfc/rfcabout.htm and http://www.fdncenter.org.

CHAPTER 6

Measuring Library Benefits
Preparing the
Survey Instruments

TO HAVE THE IMPACT THAT YOU WANT ON EXTERNAL AUDIENCES, your CBA survey results must be credible and defensible. The library director or library representative may have to defend your library's study and its conclusions. Survey reliability and validity depend not only on careful scientific sampling, as outlined in chapter 5, but on well-designed survey instruments as well. These instruments should be timed, tailored, and carefully tested to ensure good response rates, valid responses, and reliable results. This chapter reviews the structure, format, and wording of survey instruments your library can adapt for its own CBA study.

STRUCTURING THE INSTRUMENTS

Surveys should include the following sections, which we use in both our Web-based and computer-assisted telephone survey instruments:

1. Introduction
2. Dialogue about respondents
3. Benefits
4. Personal information
5. Closing comments

Introduction

The instrument should begin with a greeting and introduction. Before the survey opens in the field, the library contacts each cardholder in the sample by e-mail or letter. In that communication, the library director explains the purpose of the study and invites the household to participate. Nevertheless, the instrument itself should also welcome the respondent, confirm that the respondent is an adult, remind the respondent briefly about the purpose of the survey, and offer assurance that survey responses are confidential (though not anonymous). In a Web-based survey, the introduction should also explain to the respondent how to resume the survey if interrupted and how to change responses.

Response rates to surveys are higher if the survey engages respondents and stimulates their interest. In telephone interviews, successful interviewers establish a rapport with the respondent. Think of the instrument (or telephone interviewer) as creating a dialogue with the respondent. For these reasons, the tone of the introduction and dialogue (next section) of the instrument is important.

Dialogue about Respondents and Their Use of the Library

In the general user survey, the second section of the instrument explores the nature of the responding household and its library use. For example, how many people in the household use the library? How long does it take them to get to the library? Does the household have Internet access at home? Is there anyone in the household for whom English is a second language? The answers to these questions tailor the subsequent sections of the instrument to the characteristics of the household.

Similarly, in the survey instruments for business users or educators, this section solicits information about the users and which categories of library service they use. The answers to these questions tailor the subsequent sections of the instrument to the characteristics of the respondents.

Service-by-Service Benefits and Overall Benefits

The main body of the instrument seeks specific information on which to base the respondent's evaluation of benefits from library services. Questions in this section address in detail only those categories of library service respondents indicate that they (or members of their household or organization) use. After exploring the respondent's library use service by service, the instrument reports the value of benefits suggested by the respondent's answers and asks the respondent to affirm or modify that value. The instrument then asks a WTP contingent valuation question about the value of the library and its services as a whole. If necessary, the instrument asks the respondent to reconcile the value of benefits derived from the service-by-service dialogue and the value from the contingent valuation question.

Personal Information

Questions soliciting personal information are the last in the survey. In the general user survey, these questions address such sensitive topics as household income and members' race, age, and educational attainment. If the instrument and interviewer establish good rapport with respondents, most of them provide this information when asked in an appropriate manner. Such demographic data can enrich the library's understanding of its client base and can help the consultant explain respondents' use and evaluation of library services.

If the library has decided to combine an educator survey with the general user survey, then the instrument next addresses educators' uses of the library. This short section asks the respondent to indicate the categories of service the educator uses and follows with a question that addresses the value of those services.

Closing Comments
and Expression of Appreciation

The instrument closes by inviting respondents to offer comments or suggestions to the library director, thanking them for their assistance, and assuring them that the responses will help the library serve its community well.

CUSTOMIZING THE SURVEY INSTRUMENTS

Some libraries create their own survey instruments; others adapt instruments we have used and tested. This section explains our approach to designing instruments to measure library benefits and suggests how the consultant, liaison, and survey agency might modify the instruments to address the objectives and context for your library. Appendix C provides examples of survey instruments we used in our IMLS-funded studies to demonstrate the CBA methodology.

The General User Survey Instrument

Peruse the general user instrument in appendix C. Some changes you will make to this template are obvious. Throughout the instrument, but especially in the introduction in Section 1, insert names of your own library, library director, and survey agency. In Section 2, tailor the body of the instrument by including only those blocks of questions addressing categories of service for general users that appear in your library's service-user matrix.

Other changes are less obvious. Many of the questions about specific library services contain examples to ensure that the respondent understands the question. For the blocks of questions you include, review the examples provided and revise them as appropriate for the services provided by your library.

Consumer Surplus Questions

In Section 2, the questions that address the value of specific services embody the economic principle of substitution. They ask respondents about their willingness to purchase familiar substitutes for services provided by the library. This approach is necessary because most survey respondents find it difficult to place a value on library services directly. They have never had to pay for library services directly through a price or fee for each, so they haven't asked themselves explicitly how much a particular service is worth to them.

Placing a value on the library as a whole is even more difficult for respondents. Interviewees are especially reluctant to respond if they are asked early and abruptly in the survey instrument to provide a figure for the total annual dollar value of the library to their household. Although some respondents may have thought about the value of the library when voting on referenda for library taxes, many users simply balk if asked how much their library is worth to them overall on an annual basis. They have never had to consider the question before and find it overwhelming. Asking such a question too early in the survey instrument jeopardizes completion of the interview and the validity of the survey.

Instead, we begin by asking users to think about specific categories of library service they use. We ask them to assume that the library services are no longer available and then ask about their willingness to purchase as substitutes familiar alternative goods or services offered through private vendors. The instrument instructs respondents:

> Please answer each question based on the total amount of each service used
> by you *plus all the other members in your household combined.* If you are not
> sure whether anyone uses the service, just answer "none" or "no."

This consumer surplus approach requires that users recognize how each library service fulfills their household's needs and how those needs might otherwise be met through purchases of substitute services offered in the marketplace.

The format of a typical block of questions follows this sequence.

First, a question asks whether the household uses a particular library service and, if so, how much. If the respondent answers that the household does not use the service, then the household's direct user benefits from that service are assumed to be negligible and the instrument branches to questions addressing a different library service.

> *Example:* About how many different books for adult readers do your household members borrow per month from the _____ Library?

Next, the instrument sets up a contingent valuation scenario in which the household must consider a private market substitute and decide how much it would purchase if the library service were not available. For example, households can borrow books from the library, purchase books from a bookstore, or order them for delivery. In this example, our computer code for the price of a book purchased at a store or online is BOOKPR.

> *Example:* How many books does your household buy per month for its adult readers? (Wait for answer.) Suppose that the _____ Library was closed indefinitely due to storm, fire, or earthquake damage and could not provide the books your adult readers want. Also suppose that paperback copies of similar books are available for your household to purchase at a price of BOOKPR each. How many (if any) of the books your household borrows per month from the _____ Library would they replace by purchases at BOOKPR per book?

The purpose of the second question is to discover how much the household would increase its purchases privately to replace the library service. From this information, the consultant can calculate the value the household places on the library service.

Note that these valuation questions require the identification of an appropriate market substitute for each library service and the insertion of a price (e.g., BOOKPR above) for the market substitute. Some library services have clearly appropriate market substitutes. For example, if a family wishes to view a movie at home, the household can borrow a videotape or DVD from the library, rent it from Blockbuster or other video rental outlet, order it from a company like Netflix, or order pay-per-view. Appropriate prices for these private substitutes are the rental fees or other charges paid to such suppliers.

Other services are more unique to the library. For example, library staff "can answer questions, help people find information and materials, or suggest things to read. Staff also may help with homework, help people learning to read, or help those who have difficulty with English." Are there other ways households can satisfy these needs? Households can engage tutors to "help with homework, help people learning to read, or help those who have difficulty with English." Or, parents, friends, or other family members might spend their time as tutors instead. By asking about the household's willingness to purchase tutoring services if the library were not available, the researcher can calculate a value for this aspect of a librarian's services.

But what about the librarians who "answer questions, help people find information and materials, or suggest things to read"? Are there private-sector alternatives? Some households would pursue their questions with a search engine on the Internet. Others might use Amazon.com to search for books that fit their tastes.

Households with serious research questions (including those with professionals who need answers for their businesses) might consider hiring a private research service. For a fee, you can have these companies provide answers to questions or find information for you. They charge fees according to the amount of time it takes them to research your question. Our investigations suggest that services that are at all comparable to those available from an information librarian charge at least $50 per hour for their services.

In selecting private market substitutes, be sure to use the client's perspective rather than that of a professional librarian. From the client's point of view, the value of the library service is based on the need the service fulfills for the household. That value may differ greatly from the service's cost to the library or the value the librarian thinks the service should have.

To illustrate this point, consider the simple question of finding the spelling and meaning of a word. A librarian might suggest that this is exactly what an unabridged dictionary is designed to do. Such a hardbound dictionary is expensive. Does the acquisition cost of the dictionary represent the appropriate value to a household?

What might a household do instead? Some might go to a word processing package or the Internet with little or no additional out-of-pocket expense. Others might buy a CD dictionary or small paperback dictionary from Amazon.com or Wal-Mart. If so, the annual cost of a dictionary that probably will last five years may be little more than a dollar per year. To measure the value of library services conservatively, select the private market substitutes and their pricing conservatively.

Table 6.1 shows some of the private market services used in our general user instruments. The table also shows private market vendors offering such services and the prices they charged in 2002.

Section 2 addresses the consumer surplus method of evaluating library services on a service-by-service basis. This dialogue helps the respondent establish how and why his or her household uses the library and what the household might have to do differently if the library were not accessible.

Although these questions help the household reflect on the value of the library, the researcher should use the responses with care. Just summing the values implicit in the responses to derive the total value for all services used by the household can be misleading. In our experience, respondents overstate the value implicit in these questions for one or more reasons. They may feel social pressure, even in a Web-based survey, to overstate their use of library services and their value to the household. In addition, households have limited income. In service-by-service sequential responses about replacement spending, households do not have the opportunity to balance that spending against their other needs.

For these reasons, we have developed a follow-up question to the consumer surplus section of the instrument. Whether using a Web-based survey or computer-assisted telephone interview, the underlying program calculates the total additional outlays the respondent has said that the household would make to replace library services. Our program refers to these total outlays using the code $SPEND1, as seen in the example below. When informed of the dollar amount of that spending, respondents are often surprised and choose to reduce their answer.

> My computer has totaled the amounts you said your household would spend
> to replace _____ Library services by buying additional books or magazines
> or other services. Based on your responses, your household would spend
> $SPEND1 per year on additional purchases if these items or services were
> not available through the _____ Library. Suppose that all local taxes and fees
> to support the _____ Library were suspended during its closure. Is $SPEND1
> per year an amount your household could afford and would actually spend to
> replace _____ Library services?

The respondent may then adjust the total:

> Instead of $SPEND1 per year, how much would your household spend per
> year for additional books, magazines, and other items to replace the materials
> and services you currently use from the _____ Library?

The researchers then adjust the consumer surplus values based on the responses to this follow-up question.

Contingent Valuation Questions

The general user instrument uses two approaches to derive a value for the household's use of library services. The first measures the household's consumer surplus on a service-by-service basis. The second measures the overall value of the library in terms of the household's willingness to pay by using contingent valuation analysis. In our experience, estimates of the library's overall value using WTP contingent valuation analysis are always much more conservative and more reliable.

Contingent valuation analysis asks respondents to consider different realities, or "alternative states of the world." The WTP form of contingent valuation asks how much respondents would be willing to pay to have one state of the world as opposed to another. The WTA form of contingent valuation asks how much respondents would be willing to receive to relinquish one state of the world in exchange for another.

TABLE 6.1

Pricing of services for household survey

OFFERING	SUBSTITUTE	MEASURE	PRICE RANGE
Staff help			
Find sources of information, advise, and recommend	Information brokerage	$/hour	$10–$100
Help with homework, reading, or language	Tutor	$/hour	–
Mass-market paperback books			
Juveniles	Bookstore	$/volume	–
Adult fiction and nonfiction	Bookstore	$/volume	–
Magazines			
Domestic	Subscription	$/year	–
Foreign	Subscription	$/year	–
Newspapers			
Domestic	Per issue	$/year	–
Foreign	Per issue	$/year	–
Professional journals	Subscription	$/year	–
Electronic periodicals (general)	eLibrary	$/month	–
Electronic business and financial references	Online Wall Street Journal	$/month	–
Electronic genealogical services	HeritageQuest.com Genealogy.com Ancestry.com	$/year	$30–$190
Electronic health and fitness references	Internet		
Home reference collections	Compton's + dictionary + atlas	Purchase amortized over 5 years	
World Book Basic Reference Package	Encyclopedia, dictionary, atlas	Purchase amortized over 5 years	
Encyclopedia	Purchase	$/set amortized over 5 years	Britannica $1,295.00 Compton's $650.00 World Book $950.00
Dictionary	Purchase	$/item amortized over 5 years	$5.99
Atlas	Purchase	$/item amortized over 5 years	World Almanac and Book of Facts (paperback) $10.95

AVERAGE PRICE	SURVEY PRICE	SOURCE
$50.00	$50.00/hour	C. Berger of Chicago for experienced researcher
	$10.00	
$5.18	$5.50	*Bowker Annual* 2001, p. 488
$5.76	$6.00	*Bowker Annual* 2001, p. 470
$55.69	$60.00	*Bowker Annual*, 2001, p. 416
$165.14	$165.00	*Library Journal*, April 15, 2002
$316.60/year	$0.90/copy	*Bowker Annual*, 2001, p. 416
$1,038.86/year	$2.85/issue	*Bowker Annual*, 2001, p. 474
	$600.00	*Library Journal*, April 15, 2002
$49.95/year	$4.50	eLibrary
$72.00/year	$6.00	*Wall Street Journal*
$80.00	$190.00	Cynthia Millar, SLPL, Ancestry.com for $189.95/year
	Excluded because Web sources available for free on Internet	WebMD (free on Internet)
$700.00	$700.00	*Compton's Encyclopedia*, paperback dictionary, and paperback atlas
$1,065.00		World Book Store
		Encyclopedia Britannica, Inc., Amazon.com, World Book Store (Web)
		Border's
		Amazon.com

TABLE 6.1

Pricing of services for household survey (Cont.)

OFFERING	SUBSTITUTE	MEASURE	PRICE RANGE
Home reference collections (Cont.)			
Microsoft Encarta CD	Purchase	$/set amortized over 5 years	$34.95 for Encarta to $60.00 for Britannica
Videos/DVDs (films)	Rental	$/night	$1.00–$3.49
CDs (music)	Purchase	$/item	$7–$20
Books on tape or disk	Rental	$/rental	$3–$10
Programs			
Children	Child's theater, movie	$/ticket	$2–$13
Adults	Speaker series, live theater, movie	$/ticket	$2–$50
Computer services			
Utilization of computer	Computer rental	$/hour	$12.00
Computer training	Paid computer class	$/hour	$12–$50
Computer system without Internet		$/month for set amortized over 5 years	
Internet with modem access		$/month	
High-speed Internet		$/month	
Software: office suite	Purchase spread over 5 years	$/month	

Both our own empirical research and the literature on contingent valuation analysis show that valuation based on willingness to accept yields much higher valuations than those based on willingness to pay.[1] Clearly WTA is the less conservative approach. This is not a surprising result. If we ask people how much money they would be willing to accept to sacrifice something they already have, is it surprising that they might inflate the amount of money they demand?

OPEN-ENDED WTP METHOD

We suggest using only the WTP form of contingent valuation and not WTA. Section 4 of our household instrument contains two different sets of WTP questions. To formulate

AVERAGE PRICE	SURVEY PRICE	SOURCE
	$35.00	Microsoft Encarta
$3.49	$3.50	Blockbuster Video
$15.00	$15.00	Average retail at Amazon.com for new or popular releases
	$3.00	Cracker Barrel
$12.00	$5.00	American Theater, New Theater, St. Marcus Theater, Kid-center
	$7.50	Kerasotes Showplace12 at Edwardsville
$12.00	$12.00	Kinko's
$15.00	$5.00	Southwestern Illinois College basic introduction to the PC class, $49.00 with a $12.00 fee and $30.75 instruction booklet and CD. Consists of six 3-hr classes. Number rounded from $5.09722/hr.
$769.00	$13.00	1.3 GHz processor, 128 MB memory, 200 GB hard drive, 15-inch monitor, 56K modem, printer, cartridges, and paper for one year
$21.95	$22.00	Earthlink
$42.95	$43.00	Aliant Telecom high-speed Internet service
	$8.00	Microsoft Office XP Standard, $429 from Office Depot

questions for this format, the scenarios must first take away library services and then ask users how much they would be willing to pay to restore them. Because library services are funded through public revenues, the questions are formulated as tax referenda to restore the library after an uninsurable natural disaster.

> Suppose that the _____ Library and all its branches, buildings, books, and equipment are destroyed in an uninsurable disaster. Nothing from the library can be recovered, but no people or other buildings in your community are harmed—only the _____ Library is destroyed. A vote will be held to establish the appropriate type and amount of local taxes to restore the _____ Library and all its services just as they were before the disaster. *If the vote fails,*

the _____ Library will no longer exist. Neither your household nor other members of your community will have access to any _____ Library services. What is the maximum amount of annual local taxes and fees you would vote for your household to pay to restore and maintain _____ Library services? Please round your estimate to the nearest $100.

A follow-up question ensures that the scenarios are clear to the respondent if the respondent can't answer:

Please help us to understand why you don't know or can't answer.

If the response to the contingent valuation question (V40 in the example below) is less than the amount the household said earlier it would spend annually to replace library services (V32 in the example below), a second follow-up question asks:

You stated earlier that you were willing to spend V32 dollars per year to replace _____ Library services if the library were closed indefinitely, yet you would be willing to pay only V40 dollars per year in taxes and fees to restore and maintain _____ Library services. Please help us to understand why these answers differ.

"YES/NO" REFERENDUM METHOD

The contingent valuation literature suggests that respondents find it difficult to respond to the open-ended format of the preceding WTP question and that their responses may not be very precise. Instead, the literature suggests that respondents are more accustomed to choosing "yes" or "no" on fiscal referenda. Asking the WTP question using a sequence of "yes" or "no" referendum questions should yield more precise, replicable results. The alternative WTP question in Section 4 of our instrument illustrates this approach:

Now suppose a referendum is held to revise local taxes to restore and maintain the _____ Library so that it can again provide the same services you have today. If the referendum passes, your household would be required to pay $TAX in taxes and fees each year for the _____ Library. If the referendum fails, there would be no _____ Library. Would you vote for or against the proposition?

The value used for taxes and fees in the referendum ($TAX) is set randomly within a range of values established by the researcher.

After the respondent answers this first question, a follow-up question poses a second referendum. If the respondent rejected the first proposition, the amount of taxes and fees to restore the library is halved in the second referendum. If the respondent accepted the first proposition, the amount of taxes and fees to restore the library is doubled in the second referendum.

Suppose the referendum had a different amount that your household would be required to pay. Suppose your household would be required to pay $TAX in taxes and fees each year to support the _____ Library if the referendum were to pass. Would you vote for or against the proposition? Please help us to understand your answer.

Estimation of willingness to pay under the "yes/no" format requires a sophisticated statistical analysis and a large number of responses. In our studies, respondents occasionally commented that they felt the "yes/no" method was "sneaky." These respondents indicated that they had given a considered answer to one referendum. Then they felt manipulated into responding to a second proposition that some thought was designed to elicit a change from their first response.

The research consultant should consider the alternative techniques and their statistical requirements and decide which format to use. Do not use both formats in the same instrument. That would cause confusion during surveys and statistical analysis.

CLARITY AND CREDIBILITY OF ALTERNATIVE SCENARIOS

For contingent valuation analysis to deliver valid results, it is critical that respondents understand the alternative scenarios and find them credible. Because most citizens already have access to library services and view themselves as having property rights to the services, Aabo argues that asking library users how much they would have to receive to give up the services is more easily understood and credible than a WTP approach.[2] She wishes to measure both use and non-use value and bases part of her argument for measuring both WTP and WTA on the theory that non-use value is better reflected in WTA.

We have found that the vast majority of respondents appear to understand and accept the WTP formats offered above. Also, for individual libraries, we advocate a conservative approach that measures only direct use and excludes non-use value. Hence, our general user instruments address only WTP.

Some respondents, however, have difficulty addressing or accepting the WTP questions offered here. Concerns arise with three types of respondent: non-residents, renters, and skeptics regarding the "uninsurable natural disaster" mentioned in the scenario.

Non-residents, especially reciprocal borrowers, do not pay for services from the library under study and may not find it realistic to vote on a hypothetical referendum regarding taxes and fees for a library outside the political subdivision in which they reside. This problem argues again for either excluding non-residents from the study or analyzing their responses separately from those of residents.

Most public libraries are funded at least in part through local property taxes. Households that rent their dwellings do not pay property taxes directly. They are often unfamiliar with the size or distribution of taxes levied against the property they rent. Even though the WTP questions ask them about "local taxes and fees" as opposed to property taxes alone, renters may not understand clearly or may not believe that they will bear the tax burden implied in the proposition.

Some skeptics do not believe the scenario offered in the WTP question. These respondents often refuse to answer, or they answer "zero" to the question of how much they would be willing to pay to restore the library. In their response to the follow-up question, they raise two challenges: what natural disaster could destroy only the library, and why would the library have no insurance against it? Perhaps other researchers will devise alternative versions of the WTP question that avoid this concern.

Surveys of Other Library Users

Survey instruments for other library users should be tailored specifically to those users and the services they use. The service-user matrix should guide the construction of the survey instruments for each of these groups of users. See the second survey instrument in appendix C for an example of our business survey instrument for large urban libraries.

Of course, the instrument begins with an introduction and greeting tailored to the user group. The second section solicits information about the responding business or firm.

As in the household instrument, the main body of the business instrument contains blocks of questions that inquire about use on a service-by-service basis. The instrument pursues detailed questions only for those services the respondent indicates their business uses. For those services the business uses, the question asks whether or not the business would purchase a replacement service privately if the service were not available through the library. For example, the following block of questions addresses access to corporate reports.

Do you use library sources to access annual or corporate reports?

    ☐   No [Branch to next block of questions]

    ☐   Yes [Ask:]

What are the three most important information sources you use? Please give the actual titles if you can.

[Note to programmer or interviewer: Record the top three (unaided). But if the respondent says "don't know," "not sure," "can't remember," or something similar and cannot offer at least one reference source, prompt with the following.]

Some examples include Standard and Poors, 10K reports, and Predicasts F&S.

Then the following question is asked for each of the three services named by the respondent:

> If public libraries did not exist, would you either purchase or subscribe to or request that your firm purchase or subscribe to _____ ?

This section helps the respondent to catalog the firm's business use of the library and to consider carefully the value of each of those services to the firm.

Because these questions take an open-ended approach to the services businesses use, the responses may not have a high degree of reliability, for several reasons:

1. Respondents may not know how much it would cost their firms to replace the different services they use at the library. Consequently, they may not be able to make an informed decision about replacing them.

2. Respondents may feel that they do not have the authority to commit business funds to replace the services they use at the library.

3. Unlike the general user survey, there is no follow-up question announcing total replacement expenditures and permitting the respondent to adjust the total.

For these reasons, libraries that are confident that they know the specific services their business clients use may wish to alter the format of the business user questions to parallel those asked of general users. For example, if the library's staff knows that many business clients use Standard and Poors, the business survey might ask

> Does your firm use the library's electronic access to the Standard and Poors database?

> If "YES," then ask:

> Suppose that the _____ Library was closed indefinitely due to storm, fire, or earthquake damage and could not provide access to Standard and Poors. Would your firm choose to purchase a subscription for its own use at a rate of $__ per year?

After asking such questions for all major business services, the computer totals the outlays. Then the interviewer (or Web instrument) announces the total to the respondent and permits the respondent to reduce the total if the amount is perceived as too large.

Unlike the household survey, the business survey has no question about the value of the library as a whole. We have found it difficult to construct an overall WTP question for businesses that is analogous to the overall WTP question for general users. Why?

First, recall that the general user WTP question mimics a referendum. In the referendum, the library has been destroyed and the respondent reveals willingness to pay through a vote to raise taxes and fees to restore the library and its services. Whereas households vote in referenda, businesses do not. Furthermore, how much of the local tax burden business bears varies considerably across localities and states depending on tax law and policy. Also, business use does not recognize library boundaries. In some libraries, calls from businesses in other states are not unusual. For all of these reasons, totaling the service-by-service estimates of willingness to pay may provide a more valid measure of the library's value to a business client than a vaguely worded, confusing question about overall willingness to pay.

Business users can be difficult to contact by telephone. Even if the survey agency is successful in reaching a business, the appropriate respondent may not be available, or the respondent may need to reflect more carefully on the questions to provide useful answers. Business users may be more likely to provide considered responses to a Web-based survey than to a telephone survey.

PROGRAMMING
THE SURVEY INSTRUMENTS

Once the consultant has developed the survey instruments and the library liaison has reviewed them, the survey agency programs the Web-based and computer-assisted telephone instruments. It is important that the consultant review the programmed instruments carefully and verify that they code and record responses appropriately in a database file and format the consultant can use for analysis. Test the instruments using artificial responses that check as many of the instrument's branches as possible. The consultant should make certain that the data permit appropriate final estimates of user benefits. Errors found after the instrument is already in the field can be very costly to correct.

FIELD-TESTING THE SURVEY
INSTRUMENTS AND TRAINING INTERVIEWERS

After the survey agency programs and tests the telephone survey instrument, the survey agency and consultant train the telephone interviewers. The consultant explains the purpose of the survey, the role of the interviewers as ambassadors for the library, and protocols regarding the execution of the survey, nonresponse codes, and other such issues. It is useful for interviewers to role-play as respondents in practices delivering the instrument to each other.

As a final check on the programming and training for the interviewers, both the telephone and Web-based instruments are field-tested with a small sample of actual library users. Make sure these respondents are not in the samples of library users who will actually participate in the surveys. The library may provide the survey agency with a list of library volunteers to test the survey on the Web and to respond to pilot telephone interviews. After each test interview, the survey agency or consultant should chat with the volunteer respondent regarding the format and clarity of questions, length of the instrument, and any privacy concerns. Make changes to the instruments and test again if possible.

INVITING RESPONSES

Several weeks prior to the surveys, the library should notify those users selected to participate in the surveys. For those clients with reliable e-mail addresses, this might be accomplished by e-mail from the library director. For juveniles or those without reliable e-mail addresses, however, a letter to the patron or the juvenile's parents or guardians may be more appropriate. Formal letters are more expensive than e-mail, but your library may decide that the difference in image or greater willingness to participate in the survey is worth the cost.

The letter or e-mail from the director should provide the following information:

What: a request for cooperation and assistance in a survey of library users; only adult users or parents/guardians of juvenile users should reply

Why: a simple explanation of the purpose of the study (to measure the library's value to the community and to help the library serve the community better)

When: the dates of the survey

Who: who is administering the survey for the library and that the survey agency will ensure that all responses are confidential

How: instructions for how to access the survey on the Web; instructions for how to decline participation and hence avoid a telephone call from the survey agency

Expression of appreciation: thanks in advance for participating and a description of any gift or premium for responding if the library chooses to offer such

See figure 6.1 for an example of an invitation letter.

Send the letters by e-mail or by first-class postage so that letters with undeliverable e-mail or postal addresses are returned to the library. Keep a list of these returns to match them with cardholder records.

Date

Dear Library Card User or Parent of a Young Library Card User,

I am writing to ask you for your help. Our library is participating in an important study. Only 600 library users will be surveyed, and your name is one that has been randomly selected. This survey should take only 15 minutes of your time.

The survey will ask what library services you and your household use most and the value you place on these library services. The _____ Survey Center will conduct the surveys for the library. You can complete the survey at your own convenience through the Internet at www.xyz.com (see enclosed insert) or wait to accept a telephone call from one of the interviewers.

Of course, your responses will be handled with the utmost confidentiality. We hope that you will participate, but if you are unable to do so, please call ###-#### between 8:00 a.m. and 5:00 p.m. weekdays or e-mail us at youremailaddress@here. Please let us know no later than (date here) if you cannot participate. As a thank-you, we will send a library tote bag or small gift later to those who complete the survey.

Your cooperation in answering a few questions will help greatly in finding out about the library services you use and value. Thank you for your help with this survey and with your continuing support for our library.

Sincerely,

Ima Director
Executive Director
_____ Library

FIGURE 6.1
Sample invitation to participate

ANALYZING THE RESULTS

Calculating Response Rates

Study results are only as credible as the surveys on which they are based. Results from surveys with low response rates invite criticism that the results are biased or unreliable. A high response rate helps to mute such criticism. A well-designed and carefully executed sampling plan, instrument, and survey process maximize response. In our experience, it is possible to achieve response rates as high as 45 percent using a Web-based survey with telephone follow-up. Consultants or survey agencies may wish to review our method of calculating response rates in appendix D.

Calculating Benefits

The consultant has the responsibility of calculating the estimates of benefits and translating them into conclusions for reporting to various audiences. Consultants should see appendix E for technical discussions regarding the calculation of benefits based on the survey results.

THANKING RESPONDENTS

What our mothers always told us is still true: remember to say thank you. Very soon after executing the surveys, the survey agency should provide the liaison with a list of those cardholders who completed the surveys by Web or telephone. The library director should send a note of appreciation to cardholders and, if the library chooses to do so, a small token of appreciation or a coupon to pick up a small gift during their next visit to the library.

Respondents are often interested, too, in the results of surveys in which they participated. Consider including an article about the survey results in your next library newsletter or posting a summary of the results of your library web page.

SUMMARY

Survey reliability and validity depend not only on careful scientific sampling but on carefully designed survey instruments as well. You are welcome to adapt the survey instruments in this book to your library's study. Your survey instruments must capture and hold your respondent's interest, provide clear contexts and instructions, and elicit carefully considered responses. To ensure credibility, the surveys must have good response rates. Researchers must be able to assure audiences that the study results are representative of your library users as a whole.

Use the surveys to cultivate good relationships with library users while respecting their time and privacy. A Web-based survey offers participants the chance to respond at their convenience and at their own pace. Use telephone follow-up only for those who request it or do not otherwise reply by a reasonable deadline.

A well-designed survey opens a dialogue with your library's customers. Many library users welcome the opportunity to offer constructive feedback and even praise. They deserve our gratitude for their continued patronage, support, and counsel. Your director's letter of appreciation for completing the survey nurtures this relationship and library users' goodwill.

NOTES

1. As Svanhild Aabo comments, "Empirical WTA estimates are however often considerably higher than WTP estimates for the same good. . . . Due to this observation, and especially since the recommendation from the 'NOAA-panel' [is] to use WTP as a conservative choice . . . when the natural setting calls for estimating WTA it is instead customary to estimate WTP"; Aabo, "Valuing the Benefits of Public Libraries," *Information Economics and Policy* 17, no. 2 (2005): 175–98, available at http://dx.doi.org/doi:10.1016/j.infoecopol.2004.05.003.
2. Aabo, "Valuing the Benefits of Public Libraries."

CHAPTER 7

Measuring
Library Costs

THE PRIMARY OBJECTIVE OF YOUR CBA STUDY IS TO DOCUMENT THAT your library is a good investment of public funds. In simplest terms, you want your cost-benefit analysis to demonstrate that the value of benefits the community receives from library services is greater than the cost of providing those services. The greater the community's benefits relative to its costs, the higher the return to the community's tax support and the stronger the case for additional public funds. You also may wish to show that your library provides an impressive annual rate of return to invested capital—that is, to the physical assets the community has built up generation by generation and entrusted to the library's care. Preceding chapters addressed the measurement of benefits. This chapter explains the issues and procedures relevant to measurement of library costs.

AVOID CHARGES OF BIAS

Those directing the study may be tempted to drive the analysis to show the greatest excess of benefits over costs. "Bump up the benefits! Ignore some costs! We want our library to look great—great in comparison to other libraries and great in comparison to other agencies that compete with us for tax funds."

Perhaps Mark Twain was directing a library cost-benefit study when he commented in his autobiography: "Figures often beguile me, particularly when I have the arranging of them myself; in which case the remark attributed to Disraeli would often apply with justice and force: 'There are three kinds of lies: lies, damned lies and statistics.'" Don't succumb to Twain's temptation. Don't "arrange" the figures yourself to inflate results. To accomplish its role as a communications tool or as a guide to policy and strategy, your library's cost-benefit analysis must be defensible and credible.

Measure benefits conservatively to avoid criticisms of inflation or bias. Measure costs accurately or generously to avoid criticisms of bias. Do *not* understate costs. If the study measures benefits conservatively and costs somewhat generously, then its conclusions are conservative and defensible. Any potential critics will find little to challenge.

WHICH COSTS?

Which costs should your CBA study include? How should they be measured? The answers depend on the study's objectives and target audiences. If the purpose of your study is to advocate greater operating revenues for your library, then the study should focus on annual community benefits relative to annual operating costs. Voters, mayors, and public administrators are most interested in the return the community gets for its tax dollars. Operating costs funded from annual tax dollars should be the focus of the analysis.

If the purpose of your study is to advance a capital campaign, then your study should focus on the benefits provided through the use of the capital assets the library has built up over its history. Voters, elected officials, and public administrators want to know what return the community gets on tax dollars invested in library assets. Grant agencies and charitable foundations are interested in how their funds leverage other monies to build library assets to support library services, as well as how these services benefit the public. The leveraging of private funds with public dollars and how these outlays benefit the public should be important elements of the analysis (see chapter 8).

The task of reporting costs falls to the library itself. The external consultant can advise you but can't really collect the relevant information for you. The library's liaison to the study should assume the lead role.

Measuring Operating Costs

In a communications campaign seeking support for a budget referendum, sound bites matter. "For each $1 of annual operating support, your public library returns at least $3 in community benefits." That's a lot of bang for the buck and should impress taxpayers. How should the study measure annual operating support?

Separating Operating Outlays from Capital Outlays

The library's liaison should work with the library's financial staff to develop cost figures for the study. Conceptually, their task is to determine how much resources the library hired, purchased, or used up during the past year to generate the services and benefits the community received.

Do not include as operating costs purchases of assets that last more than one year. Those assets help provide services to the community not only in the year purchased but for years to come. They are not part of the library's current operating costs. Economists call purchases of assets with long productive lives *capital purchases* (see below).

Chapter 5 outlines measuring benefits to active cardholding households that have used the library during the past year. For comparability, measure operating costs over the same approximate time frame. The past fiscal year should be close enough. Review the library's last annual financial report or audit. It should include an income statement that lists the library's revenues, outlays, and additions to or withdrawals from cash reserves for the past fiscal year.

Consider only the outlays. If they are not already separate, filter out any outlays associated with capital purchases such as new buildings, furniture, equipment, and vehicles. Exclude any outlays for payment of debt used to fund capital purchases. Also exclude purchases that are long-term net additions to the library's collections and major software purchases that do not require annual licensing payments.

If in doubt as to whether to consider a purchase as a capital outlay or an operating outlay, classify it as an operating outlay. Be generous in your definition of costs to avoid charges of overly optimistic conclusions. The operating outlays should consist principally of salaries, including administrative and support categories, employee fringe benefits, utilities, maintenance, subscriptions, licenses, and purchases of supplies. The total of these outlays represents the operating costs used to generate library services and their accompanying benefits to the community over the past fiscal year.

Libraries that operate as administrative units of local or regional government must take special care in calculating costs. In some libraries, other government units may provide custodial, maintenance, security, accounting, repair, or other services to the library. In some libraries that receive such services, the library explicitly pays for them by transfers of funds from library accounts to the government unit supplying the services. In other cases, the other government unit may supply the services to the library with no explicit transfer of funds from the library.

If there is an explicit transfer of funds from the library, include the transferred funds as part of the library's operating costs. For example, if the library issues a budget transfer at some point in the year to cover its use of a mainframe, server, or government-owned or -operated telecommunication system, record the transfer as an operating expense just as if the library had paid an annual automation-service license to a private vendor. Do not include transfers to cover capital acquisitions, however. If the library shares in the government's acquisition of a hundred computers, then the hardware acquired falls into the capital category. Any transfer of funds associated with the purchase of the equipment should not be included in the library's annual operating costs.

If the library is not required to transfer funds to government units supplying services in kind, then the library should estimate the cost of the services supplied. To avoid understating operating costs, include an estimate of the related expenses and fringe benefits, even though paid by other government units. When considering such services in kind, ask if the library would have to pay for the service if it wasn't contributed. If it would have to, then include an estimate of the cost of the contributed service in the annual operating cost of the library.

Depreciation

The outline suggested above for calculating operating costs has one omission that some initially might consider a serious oversight. Operating costs typically include an estimate of the decline in the value of capital assets due to obsolescence, wear and tear, or other factors. Accountants call this decline in value *depreciation.*

Few public organizations, however, have accurate records or balance sheets that track the value of their capital assets. Hence, they may have little information on which to base an accurate economic estimate of depreciation.[1] Check the financial records for your library. Is there any reliable and accurate source for depreciation of buildings, furniture, equipment, vehicles, and collections? If so, review these records with your consultant to decide whether to include the depreciation figures as part of operating costs.

The methodology suggested here does not necessarily neglect depreciation, however. We recommend including in operating outlays all maintenance expenses associated with the physical plant, furniture, equipment, and vehicles. Also, in the absence of defensible measures of depreciation for collections, include in operating outlays all collection purchases that maintain the size and quality of the library's collections rather than adding to size and quality of collections. In summary, include as operating outlays any expenditures that maintain the current state of the library's capital assets rather than developing or adding to them further.

If a library expends funds to sustain its capital assets at their current level and value, then those outlays offset any true economic depreciation of the assets. Net economic depreciation of the assets would be negligible, because the total value of the assets would not decline or depreciate. Thus, neglecting to include an explicit estimate of depreciation as an operating outlay does not understate true operating costs as long as expenditures to sustain capital assets are included in operating costs.

Two examples may help to clarify the question of how to address depreciation. Consider two hypothetical libraries with different accounting practices: Our Town Library and Our City Library.

Our City Library's financial records track the values of its major capital assets, including buildings, furniture, vehicles, equipment, and collections. Its accounting practices require the library to report depreciation of these assets as an annual operating expense in its financial reports. Our City Library will include these official depreciation figures as part of its operating costs in its CBA study. It will also include maintenance outlays as part of operating costs. Its study will treat all outlays for new buildings, furniture, vehicles, equipment, and additions to collections as capital purchases and exclude them from operating costs.

Our Town Library maintains inventories of its major capital assets but has no financial records that track values of buildings, furniture, vehicles, equipment, or collections. Its accounting practices do not require any estimate or reporting of capital depreciation. Our Town Library will include as operating costs all maintenance outlays and only those purchases of furniture, equipment, vehicles, equipment, or collections necessary to sustain its current scope and quality. It will classify as capital purchases all other outlays for furniture, equipment, vehicles, equipment, or collections. It will classify expenditures to add or remodel buildings as capital outlays.

Identifying Sources of Operating Funds

Often it is useful to identify the funding sources that support the library's operating outlays. How much annual operating support comes from the public in terms of tax revenue, fees, and fines? How much comes from grants and donations?

The funding sources should appear under the financial statement's list of revenues. Segregate and total any revenue sources that are clearly earmarked for new capital outlays or debt service.

Those funding sources that are not earmarked for new capital outlays or debt service help fund operating outlays.[2] Make a pie chart showing the percentage composition of these revenues. In the pie chart, identify local public sources of annual operating funds, such as local property tax support, fees, and fines. Identify other sources of operating funds, such as grants and donations. If you desire, multiply total operating outlays by the percentages from the pie chart to find the number of dollars of operating outlays associated with each of the revenue sources.

For example, see the information for Our Town Library's CBA study in figure 7.1. In FY 2005, Our Town Library received $7.5 million in operating revenues from local taxes, fees, and fines (A.1) and $2.5 million from grants and donations (A.2) to fund $10 million in operating outlays (B). Our Town Library received an additional $7 million in revenue (C) to fund capital purchases and pay down its bonded indebtedness. Capital outlays and debt payments (D) totaled $7 million for the fiscal year. There were no net changes in the library's cash reserves in FY 2005.

The pie chart (E) shows the distribution of revenues by source. For each dollar of operating outlays in FY 2005, Our Town Library received 65 cents from local property taxes; 15 cents from state grants; 10 cents from fees, fines, and other local sources; and 10 cents from donations.

Operating Revenues and Outlays			
A. Total operating revenues			10
A.1 Operating tax support		7.5	
Property tax	6.5		
Fines, fees, and other local revenues	1.0		
A.2 Grants and donations for operations		2.5	
State grants	1.5		
Donations	1.0		
B. Operating outlays			10
Capital Revenues and Outlays			
C. Total revenues for capital purchases and debt payments			7
C.1 Local taxes for capital purchases and debt payments		5.0	
C.2 Grants and donations for capital purchases		2.0	
D. Total outlays for capital purchases and debt payments			7
D.1 Total capital outlays		6.0	
D.2 Debt payments		1.0	

E. *Sources of Operating Revenues*

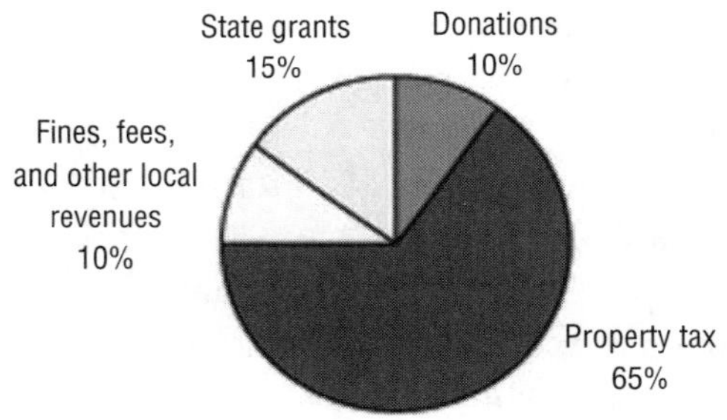

Figure 7.1
Our Town Library, FY 2005 revenues and outlays

Measuring the Value of the Library's Capital Assets

When considering rates of return on our personal investments, we are accustomed to comparing the annual flow of income from our investment against the value of the wealth we have invested. When libraries ask for support in capital campaigns, voters and foundations may find similar information helpful in their deliberations. What annual rate of return can the community expect on a dollar of its funds invested in library assets?

The public libraries with which most of us are familiar were not built in one year. Typically they are a source of civic pride that has been built up generation by generation over decades. Each generation often adds to the physical infrastructure and collections that constitute the library's assets and bequeaths to its successor a richer, more productive civic institution.

Rate of Return

The approach outlined here follows logic similar to that for calculating a firm's annual rate of return to invested capital. A firm's annual profits consist of its revenues less its expenses (exclusive of purchases of additional capital). Its rate of return is the quotient of annual profits divided by the value of invested capital. The quotient is expressed as a percentage.

The analogous concept for a library compares its annual net benefits to the value of its assets. The numerator (net benefits) is the value of annual benefits less annual operating costs. The denominator is the value of the library's capital assets.

Overstatement versus Understatement

In valuing the library's capital assets to calculate its rate of return, it is more conservative to overstate the value of the assets than to understate them. This is because a larger value for capital assets results in a lower estimate of the library's rate of return to invested capital. If faced with choices about how to value assets, select strategies that overstate asset values rather than understate them.

LACK OF A BALANCE SHEET

Most libraries do not keep accounting balance sheets that show the value of their assets, liabilities, or debts. Such balance sheets are not required of most libraries. Unlike private firms, libraries do not face the question of whether they are viable enterprises that can avoid bankruptcy and foreclosure, nor do they have to report to stockholders or financial markets. Therefore, many libraries do not track the change in the value of their net worth or assets over time.

DEPRECIATION

Often when libraries can document the value of a building or collection, it is in terms of its original purchase price. In most businesses, the value of productive assets declines over time as the productive life of the asset is depleted through use. Accountants use the concept of depreciation to capture this decline in value.

Using either original purchase price (known in the appraisal literature as *original cost* or the *book value*) or replacement cost with no deduction for depreciation typically overstates the value of a depreciable asset. With respect to the study's conclusions, it is more defensible to overstate the value of the library's capital stock and, hence, understate the return to capital. Do not use an estimate of depreciation that understates the value of the library's capital assets and overstates its rate of return.

Occasionally, however, tangible evidence of extreme physical depreciation may be overwhelming. For example, during one of our CBA presentations a few years ago, a librarian asked, "About a third of our branches are worn out. Some actually have physical hazards. How should we value those buildings in our capital assets? How should we think about depreciation?" When we reviewed a facilities study the system had done recently, it was clear that the librarian had not exaggerated.

In such a situation, carefully document in the CBA report the state of the deteriorating facilities. In putting a value on the capital assets, exclude these structures or value them close to zero. Include in annual operating costs, however, any funds spent for facilities maintenance to keep the structures open or to prevent injuries if the structures are already closed. If the old structures are having a negative effect on your operational outcomes (e.g., because the structures are so beat up or badly sited with no parking), then you ought to make this point in your study conclusions.

To reiterate, cost-benefit analysis produces a result that has to be communicated. Part of this communication is an explanation about why the study produced the particular results it did. The treatment of the capital value of such structures is a legitimate component of the defense of the study and its conclusions.

INSURANCE APPRAISALS

Some libraries carry insurance coverage for which they have to appraise the value of all or some of their assets. If so, the appraisal may be for fair market value, original cost less depreciation, or replacement cost less depreciation. With the possible exception of special collections, any of these would be defensible values to use in calculating the rate of return on the library's assets. Use of original purchase price may understate the value of special collections, however, especially for rare books that may increase in value over time. For such special collections, use an appraisal based on fair market value if one is available.

Inventorying Library Assets

The major categories of library asset are buildings and real estate, furniture, equipment, vehicles, and collections.

BUILDINGS AND REAL ESTATE

Most library buildings can be valued at replacement cost. For each building, find measurements of its usable space in square feet. Find an estimate of construction cost per square foot. Multiply square footage by the construction cost per square foot to obtain the value of the building.

Classic central branch buildings, especially those built in the Carnegie era with stone pillars, stained glass, and grand staircases, are harder to value. Fair market value is not likely to be appropriate because, in most cases, it is hard to imagine that the building would serve any purpose other than as a library unless it underwent extensive renovation. Consider evaluating such buildings in terms of replacement cost based on square footage. Do not value the building at the cost of reconstructing it with original materials and workmanship. Few libraries today would undertake such expense.

The best way to place a value on real estate is in terms of fair market value. A local realtor can provide an estimate of the selling price per acre of similar land in the same area. Multiply the lot size by the selling price per acre to obtain an estimate of value.

FURNITURE

When establishing the value of your buildings, you can find a construction cost per square foot that includes furnishing the library space. Such figures appear in the annual "building issues" of some library publications and in manuals that help librarians estimate costs of outfitting new buildings or remodeling old ones. Calculating from such a source, incorporate furniture costs with building costs. Otherwise, estimate the cost of replacing the library's existing furniture with new furniture.

EQUIPMENT

Much of a library's equipment with significant value is computer hardware and software. Place a value on the equipment on the basis of original cost or replacement cost. Note that use of original cost is likely to inflate the value of computer equipment, because the prices have declined over time.

VEHICLES

Value vehicles at their insured value or at replacement cost.

COLLECTIONS

Collections consist of hardbound books, maps, audiovisual materials, and special collections. Some libraries also have art collections. Evaluate books, maps, and audiovisual materials either at original cost or at replacement cost. If the library has an appraised value or insured value for its special collections and artwork, use it. If not, estimate the collection's market value if auctioned to private collectors. Keep notes on your methods so that you can respond to those who read or hear your study report and raise questions. Sound responses inspire confidence in your treatment of tough valuation issues and in the conclusions of your study.

SUMMARY

Cost-benefit analysis relies on a comparison of benefits provided by a public service to the costs of providing it. Credible, defensible estimates of both benefits and costs are necessary for a CBA study to perform its role as a public relations tool. Conservatively estimating benefits and somewhat generously estimating costs ensures that the study's conclusions are conservative. The conclusions provide a lower bound or floor for the library's true contribution to the community. Care taken to avoid biasing the study's results enhances the credibility of the study as a public relations tool.

Most libraries find it helpful to measure both operating costs and the value of their capital assets. Comparing annual benefits to public operating support allows a library to present its bang for the public buck—annual benefits per dollar of tax support. Using this concept, the library can formulate impressive pitches in campaigns for additional operating funds.

A library's physical assets, such as real estate, buildings, furniture, equipment, and collections, are built up through generations of public and private support. Yet most libraries do not produce annual balance sheets and do not have records of the current market value of their assets. Nevertheless, approximating the value of its assets using simple tools such as replacement cost can help a library calculate its rate of return to capital—the annual net benefits from library services expressed as a percentage of the value of the library's capital assets. Announcing the library's rate of return to its capital assets can convey to voters and donors how much current and future generations will benefit from their contributions to the library's development today.

NOTES

1. Accounting depreciation based on tax laws often overstates true economic depreciation, largely by portraying the depreciation in value at a rate much faster than the actual physical wear on the object.

2. Sometimes operating outlays are greater or less than operating revenues. If operating outlays exceed operating revenues, then the excess outlays are funded from the library's cash reserves. If operating revenues exceed operating outlays, then the excess revenues contribute to the cash reserves. If one assumes that the sources of revenues used to build cash reserves over different fiscal years are the same as the composition of operating revenues in the fiscal year used for the study, then the analysis proposed is an accurate representation of the sources of funding of operating outlays.

CHAPTER 8

Measuring Return to Taxpayer and Donor Investment in the Library

IN CHAPTERS 5 AND 6 WE DISCUSS HOW A CBA STUDY CAN MEASURE the annual dollar value of benefits the library provides directly to active library users. Chapter 7 outlines how the library can separate its operating outlays from its other expenses and identify the associated sources of funding. Together these three chapters provide the essential pieces from which to derive the conclusions of your CBA study.

Although it takes time and money to complete a CBA study like the one we outline in this book, its clear, concise conclusions make great talking points. The major conclusions of your library's analysis can be captured in one or two sound bites. Also, the conclusions are sufficiently simple that you can adapt them to convey your message to a variety of important audiences. As outlined in this chapter, the major conclusions can address benefits per dollar of operating tax revenue, benefits per dollar of operating outlays, and the percentage rate of return to investment in library assets.

In addition, prospective donors may find leveraging ratios impressive in showing how a dollar of their funds creates multiple dollars of benefits to library users. Also, library governance officials and administration should find useful the ability to know and to communicate the benefits of library use by user group, library service, library branch, or socioeconomic and demographic categories.

CALCULATING AND INTERPRETING BENEFITS PER DOLLAR OF SUPPORT

Library directors often have to defend the library's stewardship of public funds. During times of fiscal austerity, library directors may compete against other divisions of local government to defend the library against budget cuts. At other times, they may seek more annual operating revenues from tax sources by appealing to governing bodies for increases or by obtaining authorization for higher revenue through a tax referendum.

Cost-benefit analysis can assist in these situations by documenting the value of direct benefits library users receive from library services. By taking the ratio of benefits to annual tax support for library operations, the library can paint a simple, easily understood picture of the library's contribution to the community and impress upon decision makers why library services should be a priority for fiscal support.

Benefits per Dollar of Operating Tax Revenue

To derive benefits per dollar of operating tax revenue, simply divide the annual dollar value of direct benefits by dollars of operating outlays from tax-supported revenues. The numerator comes from your measure of direct benefits from chapter 6. The denominator can be derived in one of several ways, depending on the local funding and fiscal regulations of the library.

Often libraries have two distinct streams of public revenue. One set of revenue sources is clearly identified as an annual revenue stream to support operations. Another set is earmarked for capital outlays or capital debt repayment and cannot legally be used to fund operations.

If this description applies to your library, then calculation is simple. Divide the annual dollar value of direct benefits by annual public revenues to support operations. The resulting figure is the community's benefits per dollar of local tax support for operations.

If your library does not receive separate public funds for operating and capital outlays, refer again to the section of chapter 7 that addresses sources of operating funds. Apply the method outlined there to estimate the amount of annual operating outlays funded from local tax sources, such as local property tax support. Divide the annual dollar value of direct benefits by annual local tax revenues to support operations. The resulting figure is the community's benefits per dollar of local tax support for operations.

Figure 8.1 provides data for Our Town Library's CBA study. In this example, the library provided $15 million in benefits to library users during the previous fiscal year (A.1). The library received $7.5 million in tax support for operations (A.2.1). Thus, the library generates $2 in benefits per dollar of local tax support for operations (B.1):

$$\frac{\text{A.1 (\$15 million)}}{\text{A.2.1 (\$7.5 million)}} = \text{B.1 (\$2) benefits per tax dollar for operations}$$

Remember, because the numbers were calculated conservatively, this figure for benefits is a lower bound. Actual returns would be at least this great, if not greater.

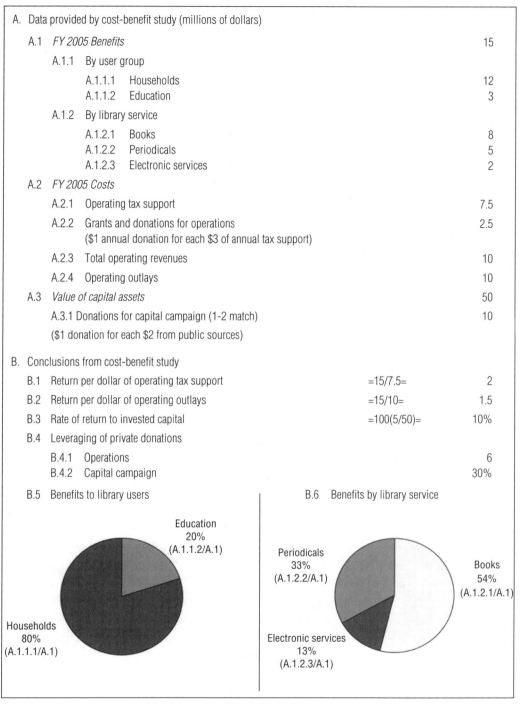

A. Data provided by cost-benefit study (millions of dollars)

  A.1 *FY 2005 Benefits*   15

      A.1.1 By user group

          A.1.1.1   Households   12
          A.1.1.2   Education   3

      A.1.2 By library service

          A.1.2.1   Books   8
          A.1.2.2   Periodicals   5
          A.1.2.3   Electronic services   2

  A.2 *FY 2005 Costs*

      A.2.1 Operating tax support   7.5

      A.2.2 Grants and donations for operations   2.5
          ($1 annual donation for each $3 of annual tax support)

      A.2.3 Total operating revenues   10

      A.2.4 Operating outlays   10

  A.3 *Value of capital assets*   50

      A.3.1 Donations for capital campaign (1-2 match)   10

      ($1 donation for each $2 from public sources)

B. Conclusions from cost-benefit study

  B.1 Return per dollar of operating tax support   =15/7.5=   2

  B.2 Return per dollar of operating outlays   =15/10=   1.5

  B.3 Rate of return to invested capital   =100(5/50)=   10%

  B.4 Leveraging of private donations

      B.4.1 Operations   6
      B.4.2 Capital campaign   30%

  B.5 Benefits to library users   B.6   Benefits by library service

Education 20% (A.1.1.2/A.1)

Households 80% (A.1.1.1/A.1)

Periodicals 33% (A.1.2.2/A.1)

Books 54% (A.1.2.1/A.1)

Electronic services 13% (A.1.2.3/A.1)

FIGURE 8.1
Our Town Library CBA study

How can we translate the result into a simple, effective statement for the media and most audiences? This result is a measure of the community's bang for the taxpayer's buck. An effective sound bite for Our Town Library might announce: "For each dollar of local tax support to operate Our Town Library, members of our community receive more than $2 in benefits from library services."

Benefits per Dollar of Operating Outlays

This measure of the library's contribution to the community is also expressed as a ratio or fraction. The numerator comes from your measure of direct benefits from chapter 6. The denominator is based on the estimate of annual operating outlays from chapter 7. The resulting ratio is the community's benefits per dollar of operating outlays.

For Our Town Library in figure 8.1, direct benefits from the previous fiscal year were $15 million (A.1). Annual operating outlays were $10 million (A.2.4). Thus, Our Town Library provides $1.50 in benefits per dollar of operating outlays (B.2):

$$\frac{\text{A.1 (\$15 million)}}{\text{A.2.4 (\$10 million)}} = \text{B.2 (\$1.50) benefits per dollar of operating outlays}$$

An effective sound bite might announce: "For each dollar spent to operate Our Town Library, members of our community receive more than $1.50 in benefits from library services."

CALCULATING AND INTERPRETING THE RATE OF RETURN TO INVESTMENT IN LIBRARY ASSETS

Both measures presented above—benefits per dollar of operating tax revenue and benefits per dollar of operating outlays—address the annual flow of benefits to the community relative to measures of annual cost associated with operating the library. These measures describe the annual net benefit current members of the community gain from the library's operation.

But a public library plays a much larger role in the community. The community will recognize that their library is also a community institution—part of their cultural heritage and a treasure for future generations. How can cost-benefit analysis capture this?

The library's buildings, furniture, equipment, and collections have been developed over time, generation by generation. These capital assets represent cumulative community wealth entrusted to the library to serve the community's citizens. The library's rate of return to invested capital expresses the community's annual net benefits from library services as a percentage of the value of these assets.

The numerator is annual net benefits, defined as direct benefits to library users less the library's operating costs. The denominator is the value of the library's capital assets as described in chapter 7. To calculate rate of return, express the ratio of the annual net benefits to the value of capital assets as a percentage.

For Our Town Library in figure 8.1, annual direct benefits are $15 million (A.1). Operating expenses are $10 million (A.2.4). Annual net benefits are $5 million (A.1 less A.2.4). The denominator (the value of the library's capital assets) is $50 million (A.3). Thus, the library annual net rate of return to investment in library assets is 10 percent (B.3):

A.1 ($15 million) – A.2.4 ($10 million) = $5 million annual net benefits

$$\frac{\$5 \text{ million} \times 100}{\text{A.3 (\$50 million)}} = \text{B.3 (10 percent) annual rate of return per dollar invested in library assets}$$

The result is analogous to interest on a savings certificate or the annual yield on an investment. Most audiences will understand the following sound bite: "A dollar invested in Our Town Library's facilities, equipment, and collections returns more than 10 percent per year in benefits to our community. That's a terrific return—better than your family could have earned by investing its own money over the past century in the best of the blue-chip stocks!"

LEVERAGING

Donors often want to know that their contributions make a difference in the quality of life in the community. Cost-benefit analysis can address this concern in several ways. First, for annual donors, the library can announce and explain its benefits per dollar of operating revenue. The return to each dollar of donations to fund operating expenses is at least this great.

Furthermore, suppose that the library can argue that annual donations effectively leverage public support, as in a challenge grant, where each dollar of the sponsor's donation is matched by additional funds from other sources. For example, if the match is dollar for dollar, then each dollar of private donations doubles the return per dollar of operating outlays. If the match is $2 from other sources for each sponsor dollar, then each dollar from the sponsor provides three times the benefits per dollar of operating outlays.

To see an example, let's return to Our Town Library in figure 8.1. Suppose the library has a revenue campaign in which private donors and foundations pledge to endow funds sufficient to provide $1 of annual endowed support for each $3 of expanded public operating revenues approved by voters (A.2.2). Then each dollar of annual endowed support leverages $4 of operating outlays. From the library's CBA study, we know that each dollar of operating outlays provides at least $1.50 in direct benefits to library users (B.2). Thus, each dollar of annual endowed support leverages more than $6 in annual benefits to the community. The director of Our Town Library could announce to prospective sponsors of the challenge grant: "For each dollar generated annually from your endowment, Our Town Library can provide more than $6 in benefits to our community."

Similarly, donors to capital campaigns want assurance that their donations contribute to the quality of life in the community, not only today but in the future. The library's rate of return to capital assets is one way of describing the annual payback from long-term investments. Furthermore, if the capital campaign is designed as a challenge, then the rate of return to each donor's dollar is the library's rate of return to library assets multiplied by one plus the matching rate.

For example, for Our Town Library in figure 8.1, suppose the director approaches a private foundation to fund a challenge grant for the library's capital campaign to build new branches and restore existing library facilities. The director proposes to raise $2 from other sources for each dollar pledged by the foundation (A.3.1). Then each dollar pledged by the foundation toward the challenge grant leverages $3 of investment in library assets. From the library's cost-benefit analysis, we know that each dollar invested in library assets provides a rate of return of at least 10 percent per year (B.3). Thus, each dollar pledged as a match by the foundation provides an annual rate of return of 30 percent in benefits to the community. The director of Our Town Library could announce to the prospective sponsor of the capital challenge grant: "For each dollar your foundation donates to our capital campaign, Our Town Library can provide an annual return of more than 30 percent in benefits to our community."

DISTRIBUTION OF LIBRARY BENEFITS

Most audiences find succinct facts like those in the above illustration sufficient for their needs. Others want more detail. For example, external funders may wish to support only one type of library service or a specific branch. Library policymakers may want to know who uses and benefits from particular services or from services at individual branch locations. They may also want to know what socioeconomic groups receive how much benefit from which library services. If you design your CBA study appropriately, your consultant can answer all of these questions with the same valid data you generated for your institution as a whole.

Distribution of Benefits by User Group

In your library's service-user matrix, your research team identifies groups of library users. Analysts can sort the survey records by user group, measure the benefits for each group, and express the results in a table or pie chart.

It is easy to translate these results into sound bites that most audiences easily understand. For example, the cost-benefit analysis for Our Town Library in figure 8.1 identifies only two main groups of library users—households and educators. The following announcement would complement the pie chart (B.5) illustrating the same conclusions: "80 cents of each dollar of community benefits from library services typically goes to households and families. The remaining 20 cents of each dollar of community benefits is generated by library services assisting educators and students in our community's schools and colleges. Not only is our library a valued resource serving our community's households and families, it is an important complement to our community's educational institutions."

Distribution of Benefits by Library Branch

You also may be interested in the value placed on the services of specific library branches. One way to plan for this type of analysis is to build an additional question into the survey instrument. Ask respondents during the survey to identify which branch or branches members of their household use. Alternatively, if your cardholder database identifies library cards by the branch where registration or card renewal occurs, then your consultant can use that information to associate survey responses with particular branches.

Using one of the two identification methods just described, your consultant can sort the survey records by the library branch associated with each survey response. Then the consultant can measure library benefits by branch and report benefits for each branch in a fashion similar to that for the library as a whole.

If the number of responses for one or more branches is small, however, be cautious in interpreting and reporting any results for those branches. Because the number of statistical observations is small, the results may have little statistical significance. Basing any conclusions or policies on such results would be very risky. Also, you don't want to be attacked for not protecting your users' privacy adequately, which could happen for a very small branch. Instead, talk with your consultant about ways to consolidate the data for small, similar branches. For example, perhaps your small branches could be classified collectively as your system's "neighborhood branches." Consolidation helps you avoid questions of statistical validity or violation of privacy while permitting you to present results for the cluster of branches as a type of library your constituents will recognize and understand.

For a variety of reasons, some branches have higher use and perhaps higher benefit value than other branches. One reason is that families—including poor families—are often highly mobile during the day. Family members go to work, to the gym, out to lunch, and to and from schools along regular travel routes within the community. Library users behave rationally. They select the branch locations that are convenient and provide the particular services they want.

The corollary of this reality is that individual library branches have different service roles. For example, some function almost entirely as "hot book" locations where users pick up and drop off best sellers, DVDs, or piles of board books for early readers. Some branches are well known for having outstanding children's departments. Others may have a strong research department. In some cases, users may elect phone or electronic access to a research department, whether in their own library system, another system, or, more frequently now, even another city via the Internet. All these factors and others affect the geographic use of individual branches.

Recognize too that, along with benefits, costs may also vary by branch. Sometimes costs are higher at a particular branch because of external neighborhood characteristics outside the library's control. For example, if management is making adequate efforts to protect staff, users, and collections at branches in high-crime neighborhoods, the addition of security staff and equipment may add substantially to the costs of those branches' operation relative to other branches. Such higher costs may be necessary for the library to provide effective access in those neighborhoods, especially if the library is committed to providing good service to poorer families who may reside there. In responses to our IMLS-sponsored surveys, we saw evidence that library users recognize and appreciate their library's security efforts. Users at several branches in difficult neighborhoods said they regarded their library branch as a "safe haven in the neighborhood." Legislators and citizens alike acknowledge the value and importance of this role for the neighborhood library, even though maintaining the safe haven adds to the library's operating costs.

Distribution of Benefits by Library Service

Your CBA survey shows how many responding households or other user groups access each type of library service. The resulting distribution can easily be shown in a bar chart relating the numbers of users to each type or cluster of library service.

Using the consumer surplus approach to measure benefits from individual library services, the analyst can calculate the benefits associated with each service or cluster of related services. The resulting distribution of benefits can easily be shown in a table or a pie chart. For Our Town Library in figure 8.1, the pie chart showing the distribution of benefits from library services (B.6) divides benefits into only three clusters of library service (suggesting a very simplistic service-user matrix). The chart illustrates the following conclusions: "Use of books generates 54 cents of every dollar of community benefits from Our Town Library services. Use of periodicals generates 33 cents. Electronic services generate 13 cents."

Estimates of benefits by library service can be useful to library managers wishing to gain insight into how to improve the allocation of the library's budget. Managers need to interpret these results with caution, however.

For example, those services with high benefits relative to their cost have great bang for the buck and may warrant additional budget or resources. Conversely, those services with low benefits relative to their cost may warrant fewer resources. But the manager should reflect carefully before wielding the ax. Are benefits low relative to costs because a particular service is new and the public doesn't know about it or hasn't tried it yet? For example, many believe that public libraries must adapt to the electronic information age and acquire and develop new electronic information sources and services. When new services are first introduced, some users may not be aware, some may be intimidated, and some may not have individual access from home or office that allows them to use the new service easily. Is a new service a failure in terms of cost-benefit analysis merely because the public doesn't yet know about it or hasn't learned to use it? The library should promote and, if necessary, educate its users regarding the advantages of any new services. The library may even have to train its users in the new service or technology. Consider carefully *why* respondents may have shown little recent use or valued a service little relative to cost before deciding to scale back the service.

Consider a second example. Your study may ask respondents about their use of library staff to answer questions, to direct students preparing assignments, to guide readers, or to suggest directions for users' own research. In our own studies, respondents' evaluations of staff services varied greatly from one library to another. Should those libraries with low respondent evaluations of benefits from staff services cut back on staff?

First ask *why* respondent benefits from staff services might be lower than expected. Has the library promoted self-service strategies for users to pursue answers so that users no longer need as much direct interaction with staff? If so, maybe fewer staff members are needed at the information desk. Maybe staff members are busy assisting users in learning search techniques and other self-service strategies, but this type of assistance was not reflected in responses to the survey questions.

Often, open-ended questions in the survey elicit responses or anecdotes that provide clues about staff problems or the need for staff development. Check responses to the survey's request for comments to the library director. Do the comments suggest that library users might be frustrated by staff attitudes or lack of training? If so, maybe the library should invest in more staff development to improve quality of service.

Also, don't forget that the library staff does much more than serve users face-to-face. Library staff members perform many other functions that benefit the user indirectly, without face-to-face interaction. For example, the staff assures prompt reshelving of materials, selects and orders new materials, catalogs materials, compiles bibliographies, mounts electronic exhibits and databases, and designs and implements new electronic services. These indirect services are part of the respondents' reported benefits under survey questions regarding use of books, media, and electronic services. The value of many staff services is implicit in user responses to these categories.

These examples point out the need for you and your staff to be active in interpreting and applying the results of your CBA study. Your economics consultant is not likely to be familiar with or aware of many issues that are unique to your library and its staff and services. Each library has many issues that only you and your particular library staff can recognize because of your knowledge about how your library system is organized and actually works. Don't rely exclusively on your consultant to interpret your CBA study for you. With careful thought and discussion, you and your staff have greater depth of perspective than your consultant alone can provide.

Comparisons of benefits by service with cost of service can help library managers formulate important questions and provide useful answers when allocation of the library's budget and resources is being considered. Nevertheless, cost-benefit analysis is only one source of information that informs the manager about the effectiveness and value of different library services. The manager must interpret these results in the light of information from other sources to make a truly informed decision.

RELATIONSHIP BETWEEN LIBRARY BENEFITS AND SOCIOECONOMIC DEMOGRAPHICS

Library managers may find it informative to ask how library benefits are related to the socioeconomic characteristics of individual households and neighborhoods. Your CBA study can summarize this information in several different ways. One way is to show how benefits are distributed across different subpopulations or constituency groups in the community. Another is to use sophisticated statistical methods to explore linkages between user demographics and library use and benefits.

Distribution of Benefits by Socioeconomic or Demographic Group

After a CBA study, a library spokesperson may be invited to present the results to particular library constituencies or to respond to community concerns regarding equity in service access or delivery. Recall that one of the last sections of our general user survey instrument asks respondents for household income, education levels, age, and ethnicity. The consultant can use these responses to describe the distribution of library use and benefits across different library constituent populations. For example, the study can report the distribution of library benefits by income class, education of adults in the cardholding household, age of adults in the cardholding household, number of children in the household, and self-reported ethnicity.

When interpreting such results, remember that a CBA study measures benefits according to what library-using households say they are willing and able to pay. For that reason, cost-benefit analysis is sensitive to differing household incomes. Library users with less income are less able and less willing to purchase substitutes for reading, literacy, and information services. With less ability to spend, the benefits they attribute to library services are likely to be less than benefits reported by wealthier families, even if the wealthier families use the library less frequently and less intensively. Except for the wealthiest households (who may purchase most of their own materials and services and rely little on the library), the CBA methodology presented here yields lower benefits per household for poor families than families with higher incomes. The methodology is also likely to show lower benefits per household at branches in poorer neighborhoods than at branches in more prosperous neighborhoods.

Does this mean that libraries that are good stewards of community tax dollars should focus their services on branches in rich neighborhoods to maximize the value of benefits to the community? Of course not. Public libraries have a broader mission.

Though the value of benefits to the community as a whole is one important element of your library's CBA study and message, making the public aware of the breadth of community participation—that is, who in the community benefits from which library services—is also very important. One reason communities value their libraries is that these public institutions offer access to educational and informational services for all persons in the community, especially families that might not otherwise have access. Demonstrating that your library not only provides community benefits in excess of its costs but also serves its less advantaged users well can be a strategic component of the message from your cost-benefit study. This can be an important message for the community at large and an important message for winning the support of critical voting blocks in the community. Work with your study consultant to frame the analysis to address strategic topics that you wish to include in communicating your CBA results.

Quantifying Relationships between Library Use, Benefits, and Constituent Demographics

How are library benefits related to the age of household members, education levels, distance to the nearest branch of the library, the household's computer equipment, number of children, income, ethnic background, and other characteristics? The consultant can use a multivariate statistical technique (multiple regression) to quantify the relationships between these characteristics and respondents' reported benefits.

Multiple regression can identify the nature of the relationship between a household characteristic and households' benefits—whether they are directly or inversely related—and test the strength of the relationship. For example, library benefits may be directly related to the number of people in the household, especially children: the more children living in the household, the greater the household's benefits from library services.

Alternatively, do benefits rise or fall with household income? Possibly, the greater the income, the more books and private services households can buy, and the less the household needs or values library services. One the other hand, the greater the income, the greater the desire for education, and the more the household may value library services. Which hypothesized relationship is correct? Or is the relationship not so simple, perhaps with a direct relationship for lower-income households but an inverse relationship at higher income levels? The statistical analysis can help the manager understand the relationship for the specific community served by the library.

Understanding these relationships can help the library manager understand how the community's support for the library might change as the community evolves over time. Will community support for the library strengthen or weaken as the population of the community ages? As household incomes change? As the community becomes more diverse? These are important questions in developing strategies for building and retaining community support over time. Statistical analysis based on the data from your CBA study can help your library understand its constituent base and plan for its future.

SUMMARY

Although designing and implementing a cost-benefit study may seem complex, its major conclusions can often be reduced to a few simple sound bites:

> For each dollar of local tax support to operate our library, members of our community receive more than ____ dollars in benefits from library services.

> A dollar invested in our library's facilities, equipment, and collections returns more than ____ percent per year in benefits to our community.

> ____ cents of a dollar of community benefits from library services typically goes to households and families. The remaining ____ cents of a dollar of community benefits from library services comes from assistance to educators and students in our community's schools and colleges.

Most audiences find such information easy to understand. Most applaud its conservative measurement as refreshing in this time when so many claims are misleading and overblown. Library directors can use these sound bites in campaigns for tax referenda, budget battles for additional operating funds, or capital campaigns to develop the library's infrastructure.

Managers may also find cost-benefit analysis helpful in internal budget deliberations and strategic planning. Benefit-cost ratios for individual services can help managers prioritize requests for additional resources. Results that report the distribution of library benefits by user group can help the library identify niche markets or geographic strengths and weaknesses. Statistical studies relating respondent demographics to benefits from library services can help managers understand how support for the library may change over time as the community evolves.

CHAPTER 9

Wrapping Up Your Study
Communicating
Your CBA *Findings*

THE INSTITUTIONAL COST AND STAFF EFFORT INVESTED IN THE planning and execution of your cost-benefit analysis makes its completion a significant event in your library's history. We recommend a few final steps to finish the project appropriately and to gain the positive attention you want.

COMMUNICATE CBA INFORMATION TO SPECIFIC GROUPS

Who Should Be Thanked?

The many staff members who worked on the project deserve a special thank-you. So, too, do the other staff who assumed additional duties to allow their colleagues to work on this special project. Several of our CBA study libraries called special staff meetings at which project participants talked about the project findings and pointed out the value customers gain from staff contacts, collections, and technology access and services. Everyone likes to feel appreciated for the work they do on the job. The completion of your CBA study is a nice moment to have a gratitude-to-staff celebration and, in the process, to encourage them in their positive behaviors.

Who Should See the CBA Study Results
First? Next? After That?

Governance officials and board members come quickly to mind as those who ought to receive special attention when announcing results. Tell them how constituents regard the library, try out your public sound bites, and offer a few user quotes from the surveys.

Besides thanking your administrative team and staff members, be sure that all members of your library organization know and understand the basic purpose, process, and results of your CBA study. When asked about the report by others (as will certainly happen), your administrators and staff should be advocates for the study and ambassadors for the library. To do this well, they must be knowledgeable and confident. You may wish to schedule department staff meetings to present and discuss the study and its results. The executive summary of the study report can assist you in conveying the study's purpose, process, and major conclusions.[1]

Perhaps docents, volunteers, friends groups, or foundations have been helping the library by their work and donations. When reporting your CBA study, point out how their efforts add value to the library's service to the community. Remember that one of the most important institutional development concepts ever devised is treating persons as "insiders." Identify organizations that have been helping your library in significant ways, such as an accounting firm that has donated its services in a special project, a vendor who has donated food for your gala, a bank that has made a series of grants, or service organizations like the Junior League or the local chapter of the National Association of Black Accountants that have assisted you in organizational development.

The completion of your CBA study is a good time to point out to the people and organizations how their generosity has contributed to the value you provide library users. Treating such individuals as insiders who receive the CBA report before it is made public will only make them feel more appreciated for the help they are giving you.

How Will You Release Your CBA Study to the Media?

Completion of a CBA study is sufficiently important to merit a brief editorial meeting to report your study results to the print media. An editorial meeting ensures that newspaper or magazine editors and reporters get accurate information about the results and unique quotes for their stories.

Create a press kit for your CBA study. For the visual media, include digital color slides and a DVD with video clips of library activities. Attach captions that demonstrate the importance of activities like these in your library's annual benefits to users and its return on taxpayer investment. If even one station picks up your "visual news release," you will gain much positive publicity—certainly more than you would have received without appropriate care and feeding of the electronic media.

If you are fortunate enough to have radio and TV stations that run public service announcements, offer to work with those media outlets to broadcast new announcements that explain how much value your library gives to the community in exchange for its tax support. As part of the announcements, point out that private-sector donations also contribute to the benefits the community receives.

How Should You Communicate with Other Specific Groups?

Above all, when planning how to present your institution's CBA report to various groups, remember that few of these groups have a comprehensive view of the library's role in the community. They see the library only through the narrow focus of their own use. If the library doesn't tell its users, governance officials, and voter publics how effectively the organization uses their dollars to deliver services to the public, these groups may never appreciate just how valuable the library's work is.

Also, tailor some of the CBA report information to non-users. How else will non-users come to know about the good job you are doing if you don't tell them? Much "library advocacy" is so general and platitudinous that it is as forgettable as a bad church sermon. Your CBA results provide an opportunity to give specific and memorable information about the value of your library to its constituencies and the community generally. Don't waste this opportunity.

How Can You Use Your CBA Results with New Donors to Raise Funds?

Since cost-benefit analysis demonstrates the value the library gives back to the community, the CBA announcement provides the opportunity to grow donors' investment in your library. Historically, libraries have been slow to build endowments. Your library's CBA results can assist you with two important tools that can help your library raise funds and build its endowment: challenge grants and planned giving.

Challenge Grants

Most libraries cultivate private donors that they hope will support the library year after year with supplementary discretionary funding. Because prospective donors often regard public libraries as a service supported primarily by taxes, they may wonder if their donations add to public funds or replace them. Challenge grants (mentioned briefly in chapter 8) avoid this confusion.

For example, if a private foundation challenges the library and its public by stating that it will match additional tax or gift support dollar for dollar, then each dollar of foundation support leverages an additional dollar of public or other donor support. *Leveraging* simply refers to the matching of additional revenue from one source with additional revenue from another. In the case of such challenge grants from private foundations, private funds clearly leverage public and other private funds.

Continuing the example, in a one-to-one challenge grant, each dollar of private support leverages an additional dollar of support from other sources. Suppose that each dollar of operating support provides $2 of benefits. Then each dollar from the sponsor of the challenge grant raises an additional dollar of other support but generates $4 of annual benefits. The return to a dollar from this one-to-one challenge grant is $4 of public benefits—a four-to-one payoff. Whether or not you decide to start a new challenge grant campaign, use the concept of leveraging to assure and encourage donors.

Planned Giving

One of the best tools to build endowments is planned giving. This legacy donation tool is in vogue right now because of the trillions of dollars that will pass from one generation to another as the baby boomers die and pass on their accumulated wealth. Recognition of this huge forthcoming bequest of wealth is fueling the many current heated policy debates over repealing the inheritance tax.

Planned giving comes in many varied forms and has substantive policy implications for your institution. Implementing planned giving requires a degree of expertise that cannot be picked up by reading a single book or buying an inexpensive package of materials (one of hundreds available) on the Internet. Like other financial and legal matters, spend some of your time and some of your library's funds to research which planned giving strategy will work best for your library.

No matter how you decide to implement planned giving, your CBA study can help you market your library to prospective donors. Remember that your study documents your library's return on investment. If your library shows an impressive return on public investment, you have a powerful, conservatively constructed statistical statement to illustrate the impact created by endowed funds provided to the library through legacy giving.

HOW OUR IMLS LIBRARY PARTNERS
USED THEIR CBA RESULTS

Challenge grants and planned giving programs may be institutional strategies that are still in your future, but the CBA studies we did—and the one you will do—can have immediate benefits. The list that follows shows how libraries that participated in our IMLS-funded CBA studies used their study results to make immediate, verifiable, positive changes.

> Several participating libraries used their CBA results in persuasive appeals to governing bodies and voters that highlighted the need for additional funding.

Several participating libraries used a breakout page showing the dollar-estimate household benefits to specific groups of general users by resource type. One library's page, for example, showed that 81 percent of all households benefited from "books for adults," and 62 percent benefited from staff "research help." Electronic materials were also important in the total benefits package, with 12 percent of users receiving benefits from "computer usage," 17 percent from "educational software," and 30 percent from "music CDs for adults." (DVDs were just beginning to appear in the marketplace when this survey was taken.) In other words, library leaders could see which materials and services produced the largest streams within total benefits. This analysis led to a great deal of thoughtful discussion among staff (like that discussed in chapter 8), and it led to resource reallocation in the annual budget as well. Those who made such changes, we are certain, would tell you that it was useful to actually have measures of how library users valued individual services. Such evidence, though far from an absolute on which to base a budgetary decision, is far better than no evidence at all.

One participating library used the study to demonstrate how it was balancing traditional materials and services with recent innovations in materials and services. This educational program was used with both staff and library users to show how the library was adapting to changes in technology and customer service desires.

A participating library used its study results to "Let . . . Staff Know How Great They Are." The CBA study results were integrated into staff training with the specific intent of raising staff morale.

A participating library dramatically increased the institutional training budget because its CBA study results demonstrated how valuable staff was. The director recognized that greater investment was likely to increase their value and that spending more money on the library's most critical resource made more sense than putting it somewhere else in the services budget.

A participating library was able to break out the benefits of the work of a library cooperative not only for general users but for educators and business users as well. This same library prepared a presentation that showed a slide titled "What we learned." The bullets: "Gained new understanding of user base; reaffirmed the value of staff to the users; and raised the staff's self-esteem."

A participating library that encountered problems when we tried to sample its user database used the experience to reform its registration and card-updating feature.

SUMMARY

Planning how to communicate the results of your library's CBA study is just as important as planning the study itself. Your CBA study can be an important internal decision-making tool, but it can also serve important strategic objectives with external audiences, including advocating for more public or private funds. Communicate your results clearly, confidently, and strategically to achieve your objectives.

Our past library CBA studies have served participating libraries in many ways and helped them communicate with a wide variety of audiences. These CBA studies not only provided ammunition for better political communication about the benefits of library use but also furnished statistical evidence to help libraries make their services more efficient and more effective. We believe it is fair to say that, as more libraries undertake CBA studies, they will discover innovative and legitimate new uses for the results produced by this analytical tool.

NOTE

1. For a sample report, see http://www.ala.org/editions/extras/Elliott09232/.

CHAPTER 10

Conclusions
Evaluating What Your
CBA Study Accomplished

AT THE COMPLETION OF EACH OF OUR FIFTEEN STUDIES IN FOURTEEN different libraries, we evaluated our research methodology and our results. If you read in sequence our project publications, listed under "Additional Reading" in chapter 1, you can see how we changed elements in the methodology throughout the project. A major innovation was creating an online survey option for one of the libraries involved in the second IMLS-funded study. Another was refinement of the calculation of operating costs and the valuation of library assets. Because we studied many different libraries, we had to modify our methodology to ensure that it was transportable and could address the huge variations in accounting systems, collection ages and types (including some large rare book collections), building types (monumental to intentionally inexpensive), and choices and emphases in services.

Throughout the studies, however, we maintained our conservative approach to every aspect of the methodology associated with estimating benefits. Using conservative pricing of private-sector substitutes and counting benefits only where we could find a substitute product in the private sector are just two examples. In other words, we evaluated performance throughout our project and made changes to refine and improve the methodology.

BENEFITS OF THE CBA STUDY:
WHAT PARTICIPANTS SAID

Within this context of ongoing project evaluation, we asked participants at each library to assess the outcomes of our research. Specifically, we asked them to consider benefits our CBA studies had provided for their institutions and for the federal taxpayers who funded much of our research.

Project teams from each CBA study library responded to a brief evaluation survey. In some cases, we intentionally asked participants to complete their surveys many months after we had completed our project in their library so that they could consider carefully how they had used their study. Participants responded using a scale of 1 through 5, with 5 at the top and 1 at the bottom, in blanks in front of statements describing different possible outcomes. We obtained the following general conclusions:

> By and large, every participant in every study agreed that they better understood their institution and were better able to make positive changes in its operations after completion of the CBA study.

> The construction of the service-user matrix and the corresponding measures of benefits in the study led library personnel to a greater understanding and appreciation of the library and its services from a customer perspective.

> The results of the CBA study helped board members and administrators see the relationship between specific user groups, such as households and educators, and the value each group placed on library access and service.

> The results of the CBA study helped executive directors make more informed budgetary decisions. The study informed resource allocation by quantifying the benefits of particular services for comparison against their costs.

> The results of the CBA study were informative to library staff, helped boost staff morale by demonstrating the value of the library to the community, and impressed upon executive directors and administrators the importance of staff training to effective customer service.

> The CBA methodology provided a "defensible floor" for the estimated return on public investment in library services.

> The results of the CBA study were valuable to the libraries in their external public relations. The study quantified the libraries' value to their communities in a manner that was persuasive to external audiences such as local governments, donors and foundations, and taxpayers.

> The concept of the return on taxpayer investment assisted libraries in illustrating the benefits of private-public financial partnerships, such as private-sector gift or grant programs to leverage library services beyond those paid for by taxes.

> Participation in the CBA study often caused a library to reevaluate the effectiveness of its practices and information systems used to maintain and access its cardholder database.

Participants viewed the CBA methodology as transportable to other libraries the same size or larger than those included in the studies.

The research produced a policy tool worth the investment of federal tax dollars and their libraries' time and effort.

When you finish your CBA project, we hope you will use criteria like these to evaluate the outcomes of your own study.

LIBRARY STATISTICAL MEASUREMENTS AND THE ISSUE OF ADDING VALUE

Thoughtful leaders who operate library organizations gather statistics for two reasons. One is to make or affect policy. It is a cliché but still valid to cite the old business saw, "If you can't measure it, you can't manage it." Always eyeing the future, the best library leaders identify, define, and collect whatever statistics will help them improve their institution's operations and increase the benefits the organization's operations provide directly to its users and indirectly to the larger society.

The second reason is to measure what a library has accomplished. Here we run head on into issues inherent in traditional library statistical measurements. Library statistics are based on an industrial-production system involving inputs and outputs. What this system tells us in simplest form is whether a library has "produced" as many units this month or this year as it did in the last comparable periods. In that context, borrowed as it is from industrial factories, we think we have done "better" when we increase outputs while keeping output costs the same or even lowering them. In business terms, we have increased productivity and operational efficiency. Much of the HAPLR Index and most other library ranking mechanisms are based on this industrial production model.

Libraries can and do calculate what services cost to produce. Libraries can and do count how much services people use. But except for our calculated costs, we have practically no idea what a library's product is worth to the end users in our communities. We can be very efficient in delivering our services and holding down costs, but if we as managers have little sense of the value we contribute to the community, then why would we expect our community to invest further in our libraries? In short, we have no way of telling, in monetary terms, how much value our work adds to the lives of those we serve. But shouldn't this be an essential question in managing our libraries?

In the private sector, managers use productivity measures to ensure "value added" to the product by the manufacturing process. By managing productivity efficiently, the manager ensures that production occurs for the least cost. Given the price consumers are willing to pay for the factory's product, the manager can then adjust the factory's production level to maximize the operation's profits.

Both the private-sector manager and the library manager are concerned about productivity, efficiency, and costs. The key difference between private-sector managers and library managers is that private-sector managers confront the consumer's willingness to pay for every good or service they deliver. They have to meet the test of the market and the market price with every transaction. With each transaction, they see the value consumers place on their product.

Library managers, however, do not sell their libraries' services to consumers. Libraries do not face the test of prices determined by the markets—prices that reflect consumers' willingness to pay. Since the libraries' industrial production/input-output statistics focus only on productivity and costs, such statistics cannot function as an analytical tool to gauge how end users value the services the library produces.

There was no problem in this explanatory gap until our society began to ask its public institutions to justify themselves. Just like most other federal agencies, IMLS operates under the 1993 law that requires federal agencies and those that take federal money to measure the outcomes that occur because of their expenditure. At the same time, local and state political leaders—all of whom take federal money in one form or another—decided to adopt the federal output guidelines and include state and local expenditures under the same terms. Whenever that happened in your state or locale, your public library had to begin articulating its case that its public funding created a documented net benefit for your community.

The flurry of recent library statistical studies with the word "benefits" in their titles should be examined within that context. Our study is one of these. It was no accident that we began our study in 1994. The federal "outcomes demonstration" requirement already had made its impact in the minds of some library directors. When they made their desire for a tool to measure dollar benefits known to a member of our research team, we began our effort to apply cost-benefit analysis to public libraries. The fact that other research teams are publishing "benefits studies" has conditioned the writing of this book. To ensure that our readers can contrast the methodologies, we have reported carefully all the realities of using our methodology, including its assumptions, limitations, and opportunities.

Our application of CBA methodology has produced results that build on available library statistics supplemented with new survey data in which users not only report on what they use but place a value on that use. The study methodology then reports on the customers' specific uses of their library and the value they attribute to their use.

In so doing, cost-benefit analysis examines the outcome of the total relationship between a library and its customers. In the process, cost-benefit analysis ties the value users set on those transactions to the public dollars the library spends to sustain those services. In an elemental form, it ties public dollars to customer behavior—and thereby provides a conservative economic measure of the value of the library.

Reporting that relationship, analyzing it, and making different policy decisions because of such a study are part of what strategic thinking—and strategic planning—are all about. Within such a perspective, undertaking a CBA study and reporting that study's outcomes can become a positive learning experience for the whole institution. It is another tool for teaching the institution about itself and thinking about where it wants to go.

THE SEARCH FOR THE SILVER BULLET

Those who know anything about how to kill werewolves or how the Lone Ranger saved the American West from bad guys are familiar with the mythical power of the silver bullet. Whether the enemy was werevolves or bad guys, its legendary powers were magical.

We raise the mythology of the silver bullet in this report on the economic study of libraries because, over and over through our CBA research, we heard articulated the desire for a silver bullet. One such desire goes, "All we want is a formula where we can plug in our library statistics and we will get a figure back that shows all that value we give to the community." Another seminar attendee put her interest in a shorter form: "Give us the magic bullet, the one or two phrases that will make funders give us more money." If only social science research, fund-raising, and politics were so easy.

At the San Antonio Midwinter ALA Convention in January 2006, the largest organization of American libraries handed out thousands of brochures titled "ALA Ahead to 2010." The upper-left column material from "Ahead to 2010" reads as follows, with the numbered sequence being the first three of the stated six "strategic objectives."

GOAL AREA 1:
    ADVOCACY/VALUE OF THE PROFESSION

GOAL STATEMENT:
    ALA and its members are the leading advocates for libraries and the library profession.

STRATEGIC OBJECTIVES:
1. Increase support for research and evaluation to provide evidence regarding the value and impact of libraries.
2. Increase public awareness of the value and impact of libraries of all types.
3. Increase public awareness of the value and impact of librarians and library staff.

These strategic objectives reflect the intense interest of the ALA, the PLA, and hundreds of individual libraries, library consultants, and library leaders. All want a simple formula—a shortcut advocacy statement into which they can insert a few input and output measures, enter some base dollar figures from the annual operating budget or some capital investment statistics, and get back an advocacy statement that illustrates that libraries are a great investment and that they deserve more funding when compared with all other public services.

Our methodology is not one that produces a valid value statement with so little effort. Nor is it a methodology in which you can apply the results from one library's cost-benefit analysis to another library merely because it has similar input and output statistics. As we pointed out earlier, input and output statistics focus on productivity and efficiency, not on value. Value varies with many other attributes of the library, its services, and the community it serves. We have seen this systematic variation clearly and can demonstrate the variation statistically in the data from our fifteen studies. If our methodology is used for a study for a particular library, the results are unique to that library. Only that library can use the results for advocacy. The methodology we devised and tested for large and medium-sized libraries is transferable to other libraries; the statistical results from one library study, however, are not transferable to other similar libraries with similar input and output statistics. Such a transfer is methodologically invalid.

Until additional studies of a wide variety of individual libraries are completed using sufficiently similar methodologies, the research needed to generalize results to other libraries with statistical confidence is probably impossible to conduct. Current data are simply statistically inadequate. Such a "meta-analysis" will have to wait, no matter how eager library professionals are today.

We recognize that ALA in its newest strategic plan is attempting to find easily applicable benefits formulae. So, too, are other organizations. One notable example is the Americans for Libraries Council, which in November 2005 sponsored a conference to review such methodologies, including the one we developed. The title of this conference reveals its purpose: "The Art of Library Valuation Studies: Building the Business Case for Public Libraries."

We do not believe that any of the research models presented by various teams at that conference should be used for advocacy by groups other than the specific research subjects. If executed properly, valuation is site-specific and not transferable to other locations. Methodologies may be transferable. We have demonstrated fourteen times that our methodology is.

As clearly as possible, we as a research team state that, unless library professionals take the time and go to the expense of carrying out statistically valid studies to support their research, the profession should abandon the idea of a simple pocket calculator. To any informed economist, an "impact study calculator for the arts or for libraries" is a joke. No respected economist will find it credible or consider it anything but a simplistic sales gimmick. Eventually it will be discredited as nothing more than sheer boosterism. For librarians to go down that road would be a huge mistake. Using a faulty measurement instrument does not add credibility to any statistical claim or serve the library profession.

SUMMARY

This book presents a research methodology, cost-benefit analysis, as applied to large and medium-sized public libraries. It includes a detailed explanation of how this CBA methodology can be replicated by other libraries to establish the value of their services to direct users. It includes examples of work documents that we developed and used successfully in these studies. These include complete survey schedules of the "question trees" for interviewing general users and business users. We have accomplished what we set out to do: we have created a transferable methodology that other researchers can apply and adapt to meet the valuation needs of the library systems they are studying.

Better than anyone else, we realize the issues our studies have raised. It costs money to do good research. Statistical research is never cheap if done right. And econometric research in any public setting, including public libraries especially just now in their history, is bound to have controversy associated with it.

We encourage continued economic research on library services valuation. There is, however, more work to be done. Now that ALA has focused on statistical valuation, perhaps the size of the LIS statistical community can be grown and additional public economists can be persuaded to set their research sights on libraries. In the meantime, we return to where we started. To those of you who have picked up this book because you may want to try a CBA study of your library or library system, we encourage you in your effort. When you have completed your study, we are certain that you will find the benefits of the knowledge you have created of enormous use in improving the value your institution gives to the community.

Measuring Consumer Surplus
by Contingent Purchases of Substitutes
A *Technical Appendix for Economists*

TO ILLUSTRATE THE MEASUREMENT OF HOUSEHOLD BENEFITS FROM LIBRARY services using the consumer surplus approach, consider households that borrow books from their local library. Patrons may borrow books from their local library or purchase books from Amazon.com or their local bookseller. Most patrons do both. Figure A.1 shows a patron's demand for borrowing library books. Even though borrowing privileges are free to system residents, the patron faces an average transaction cost tl in accessing the library. The diagram on the right shows the patron's demand for purchasing books. At a gross price of $P + tm$, where tm is the transaction cost of purchasing a book, the patron purchases $QM1$ books per period in addition to borrowing $QL1$ books per period from the library. Borrowing books and purchasing books are close substitutes. Although the gross price of borrowing is usually less than the gross price of purchasing a book, sometimes purchasing is more convenient (lower gross cost due to lower transaction costs), satisfies a more urgent need, or satisfies the need for ownership of the book. This explains why many households both borrow and purchase books.

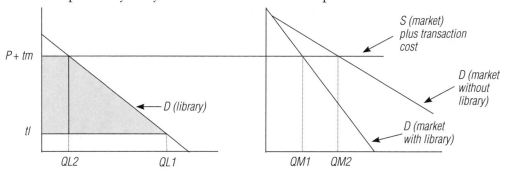

FIGURE A.1
Markers for library services and private-sector substitutes

If their local library did not exist, patrons would face a price of $P + tm$ for all access to books. This former library patron would add $QL2$ books per period to the market demand of $QM1$ for a total of $QM2$ books purchased per period. The consumer surplus for library borrowing privileges would be the area of the trapezoid lying under $D(library)$ between tl and $P + tm$. For simplicity, we assume that tl and tm are approximately equal. If the library did not exist, the change in price of books the patron otherwise would have borrowed would be $P + tm - tl = P$. Hence, the consumer surplus is the area of the trapezoid, which is equal to one-half of the product of P and the sum of $QL1$ and $QL2$.

In practice, to measure the benefit of a specific library service, we identify a close market substitute for the library service, determine the price of the substitute, and survey patrons in contingent analysis to measure $QL1$ and $QL2$. $QL1$ is factual: "How many books does your household borrow per month from your local public library?" $QL2$ is counterfactual: "If your household could not borrow books from your local public library, how many more books would your household purchase each month at a price of $\$\_\_$ each?" Given the responding household's answers, we can calculate consumer surplus for the library service.

Sampling Cardholders

REQUEST TO THE LIBRARY'S DATABASE SUPERVISOR:

Our library is launching a project that will estimate the value our patrons place on library services. A survey of a carefully selected random sample of current library users is critical to the validity and reliability of this study.

You and your staff will prepare the sample of library users for this study. In preparing your sample for the project, it is important that you complete the following steps in order. Think of your responsibilities to the project as consisting of three stages: (A) collaborating on a sampling design, (B) extracting a test sample, and (C) executing the timely extraction of the survey sample when requested to do so.

Steps I through III in the instructions below relate to stage A, collaborating on a sampling design. Once our study liaison and consultant have accepted the sampling design, proceed to steps IV and V, which apply to stage B. These steps outline how to draw a test sample, format the records into a file, and ship it to the consultant. The test sample will help you understand how to draw the final sample later in the project and will help the consultant see how your data will be organized.

For stage C, the final sampling you will execute months from now, timing is critical. For the survey to be successful, the records must be current and complete. The sample must arrive "just in time" to avoid delaying the survey. Our library's project liaison will give you the timeline for the survey and the due date for your sample. You will need to repeat steps I, II, IV, and V in extracting the survey sample. Step III will not have to be repeated for the final sample.

Your skills and efforts are essential to the successful completion of this project. We value your efforts and welcome the opportunity to collaborate with you. Please contact the liaison or the project consultant with any comments, questions, or suggestions.

Step I. Define cardholder population.

    A. Identify current users.

        1. Select only cards used in the past 12 months, whether for circulation or for electronic access.

        2. Exclude all library staff, both full-time and part-time.

    B. Screen out duplicate addresses.

        1. Where two addresses are the same, in deciding which card to keep:

            a. prefer cards with valid telephone numbers (see 2 below).

            b. prefer cards of adult cardholders to those of juvenile cardholders at the same address.

        2. Count and report to the study liaison and research consultant the number of records after eliminating duplicates. Label this number as the "count of active households" in the cardholder population.

Step II. Screen out records with a missing, incomplete, outdated, or invalid telephone number.

    A. Because the surveys will be administered by telephone interview, it is critical that each of the records you submit has a current, valid telephone number.

    B. Where possible, update phone numbers prior to sampling for the survey.

    C. Check phone number fields for

        1. correct number of digits.

        2. area codes appropriate for your service region.

        3. prefixes active in your service region.

    D. Count and report to the study liaison and research consultant the number of household records eliminated due to problems with the telephone number field. Label as "count of records invalidated by telephone field."

Step III. Stratify by geography, type of card, and/or intensity of card use.

    A. The purpose of stratification is to make the sample as representative as possible with respect to important aspects of your cardholder population.

    B. Working with your consultant and project liaison, begin by identifying critical characteristics of the cardholder population for which you have information in your database.

        1. What information does your library record about each cardholder?

            a. Are cards designated to branches?

            b. Does your database distinguish between residents and non-residents? If both, should the survey include only residents, or residents and non-residents?

            c. Are cards classified by geography or type of user?

            d. Does the card record contain an e-mail address?

e. Does your library offer different library cards or privileges to different classes of cardholders—e.g., adult, juvenile, business, teacher? If so, how are classes of cardholders identified on the card record?

f. Does the card indicate the number of transactions during the past year? The date of the most recent transaction?

2. What "niche markets" do you serve? Are there particular groups of patrons for whom the library offers special programs or services? For example, does your library promote special services for particular local schools, local businesses, a nearby military base?

C. Your consultant and study liaison will select only two or three characteristics to form strata (i.e., user characteristics that help us ensure that the sample is representative of your library users). For example, suppose that we stratified based on ZIP code and the presence or absence of an e-mail address.

1. Using ZIP code to stratify can help us ensure that our sample is representative geographically (which may also correspond to socioeconomic characteristics of our cardholders).

   a. If you have cardholders in more than three ZIP codes, sort by the two largest and group records from all other ZIP codes into a third geographic area.

   b. You could perform a similar stratification with resident versus non-resident cardholder records instead of ZIP code.

2. Using the presence of an adult's e-mail address can help us ensure that our sample is representative with respect to the technological preferences of our cardholding households.

3. If we have three ZIP code categories and two e-mail categories (e-mail address or no e-mail address), then we can sort the household cardholder records into six strata. Suppose that we have 5,000 household records:

ZIP code 1 with e-mail # of records: 1,000 Proportion: 1,000/5,000=20%	ZIP code 2 with e-mail # of records: 500 Proportion: 500/5,000=10%	ZIP code 3 with e-mail # of records: 500 Proportion: 500/5,000=10%
ZIP code 1 w/o e-mail # of records: 1,500 Proportion: 1,500/5,000=30%	ZIP code 2 w/o e-mail # of records: 1,000 Proportion: 1,000/5,000=20%	ZIP code 3 w/o e-mail # of records: 500 Proportion: 500/5,000=10%

D. Report e-mail definitions of the strata and counts for each stratum to the project liaison and consultant before proceeding to the next step. Give them time to respond to this information regarding the stratification design before you proceed further.

E. This information is important to the research project so that the researchers can test and correct for nonresponse bias after the survey is completed.

Step IV. For the test sample, using random sampling, select 2 random samples of 50 records each. For the final survey sample, when instructed to do so, select 50 random samples of 50 addresses each (total 2,500).

A. Sort the household records into strata (see III above).

B. Divide each record count in each stratum by the total number of records. This will give the proportion of each sample of 50 that you should draw from each stratum.

1. For example, suppose that the stratum "ZIP code 1 with e-mail" in our stratification described in III-C above has 1,000 records of the 5,000 records in the household population. Then 20 percent of the active cardholding households live in ZIP code 1 and use e-mail. In each sample of 50 households, 20 percent should be drawn from that strata: draw 10 records from that stratum for each sample of 50 records.

2. Draw the records without replacement. In other words, once you select a record for one sample of 50, do not permit that record to be drawn in any other sample of 50.

C. After selecting samples of 50 records each, assign ID numbers in consecutive order 1–100 for the test sample or 1–2,500 for the final survey sample. ID numbers 1–50 would designate sample 1 of 50 records, ID numbers 51–100 would designate sample 2 of 50 records, and so on.

D. For the test sample, print addressed envelopes for the first 10 sample records only. For the final sample, you will print all 2,500 addressed envelopes based on your final sampling. Your library director knows that we have requested these envelopes along with 2,500 sheets of letterhead. We will provide further instructions regarding the letterhead and envelopes at a later date.

Step V. Create electronic files.

A. Create an Excel file for the sample records:

Type of information in field	Essential field? (Cannot be missing or blank)	Notes
Library name	Yes	Use abbreviation, such as SLPL for St. Louis Public Library.
ID number	Yes	See IV-C above. Do not include commas.
Card number	Yes	Library card number. Note that field format permits alpha or numeric characters.

Greeting	Yes	Adult record: Mr./Mrs./Ms./Dr., etc. Juvenile record: "Parent or guardian of."
Name of cardholder	Yes	First name of cardholder followed by space followed by family name.
Address	Yes	Can include ZIP code, but ZIP code must also be entered as separate field.
ZIP	Yes	Five-character ZIP code.
Telephone area code	Yes	Check to be sure that all records have area codes that are valid for service area.
Telephone number	Yes	No hyphens or dashes or parentheses. Check to be sure that all prefixes are valid for service area.
Cardholder e-mail address		Adult cardholder's e-mail address if included in library database.
Adult or juvenile card		A = adult J = juvenile
Resident or non-resident		R = resident N = non-resident
Other local stratifier 1		Field to identify other data used to stratify records.
Other local stratifier 2		Field to identify other data used to stratify records.

B. Compress your data into a zip file.

C. Write an e-mail message containing the following:

1. Library name

2. Name of person responsible for database and sampling

3. Contact information for that person:

a. E-mail address

b. Phone

c. Fax

4. Identification and definition of stratifying variables

5. Population counts of households in each stratum on the date of the sample

6. The date on which the sample was drawn

D. E-mail with compressed data file to both the project liaison and the consultant.

Survey Instruments

HOUSEHOLD SURVEY INSTRUMENT

This appendix illustrates questions embedded in the Web-based and telephone survey instruments used in our IMLS-funded studies of public libraries. The actual survey instruments are computer programs. These programs employ skips, loops, automated prompts, and randomized order for some questions. The instruments also calculate certain totals based on respondents' answers, employ the totals in consistency checks, embed the totals in follow-up questions, and store responses in a computer database for later processing and analysis.

We have selected the telephone survey format to illustrate the questions and interview protocol. The text below contains both standard font and italicized font. The standard font contains instructions for interviewers and programmers. To read the script of the survey as an interviewer would, read only the bold italicized sections and ignore the instructions. Underscored words or blanks indicate information that would be inserted by the program, including such information as the name of the library and the prices of various items or services (prices have a PR suffix).

Almost none of the respondents to our surveys answered all the questions in the instrument. For example, households without children do not answer questions about children's books and programs. Households with no nonnative speakers do not answer questions about foreign periodicals. We have left some programming instructions in the instrument below to give a sense of how respondents' answers direct the flow and length of the interview.

Though it is not appropriate to provide a comprehensive discussion of the programming dynamics of the instruments here, we hope that the instructions in the standard font below prove helpful to those who wish to design and program their own instruments.

Initializing Interview

■ Screen should instruct interviewer to click via drop-down windows: date, time, interviewer name, and supervisor name.

■ Upon exiting this screen, the computer should display the telephone number for the record.

Introduction

Hello, _____, Director of the _____ Library, asked that I call. May I please speak to _____?

■ If no answer or if answering machine, show screen with callback message for answering machine. Record date and time of call, termination status, and proceed to the next prospective respondent.

■ If no respondent is at home who can speak English, show screen to terminate the call and instruct interviewer to mark the record as NO ENGLISH.

My name is _____. I work for _____ survey agency. As part of a sponsored research project, we have been asked to interview households who use the _____ Library. Did you receive Director _____'s letter explaining this research project?

■ If "Yes," continue the interview with screen showing next bullet.

■ If "No," show screen saying:

We are talking with library patrons or their parents to see which library services they use and how much they use them. Your responses will help us evaluate and improve your library services.

I assure you this is a confidential survey. Your responses will help the library understand how your household uses library services and how to serve you better. May I take about 15 minutes now to ask you some questions?

■ If "Yes," show screen with next bullet.

■ If "No," show screen saying: *May I call you later at a more convenient time?*

   • If "No," show: *Thank you for your time, good-bye.*

   • If "Yes," show: *What time would be convenient?* (Record day and time _____, and follow up when appropriate.)

Because you will be responding for your household, we need to know if you are at least 18 years of age.

   ■ If "Yes," go to Section 1.

   ■ If "No," show screen: *May I speak to your parent or guardian, please?*

      • Start interview again. *May I ask your name, please?*

      • If no responsible adult is available, say: *When would be a good time to call back?* (Record day and time _____, and follow up as appropriate.)

Section 1

First, we would like to know about people in your household and how they use library services.

1.1. ***Has someone in your household used their library card during the past 12 months?***

   □ Yes   □ No   [If "no," thank respondent and terminate interview.]

Does anyone in your household use _____ Library services

1.1.1. ***by computer from home or work?***

   □ Yes   □ No

1.1.2. ***by visiting a bookmobile?***

   □ Yes   □ No

1.1.3. ***by going to _____ Library?***

   □ Yes   □ No

1.1.3.1. If V113=1: ***Approximately how many minutes does it take people in your household to get to the _____ Library—a one-way trip?***

   _____ minutes

Please help us to understand who lives in your household.

1.2. ***Are there any children under 18 in your household?***

   □ Yes   □ No

1.2.1. If V12=1: ***How many children are under age 5?***

   _____

1.2.2. If V12=1: ***How many are 5–13 years old?***

   _____

1.2.3. If V12=1: *How many are 14–17 years old?*

_____

1.2.3.1. If V122+V123>0: *Does anyone in your household homeschool any of the children who live with you?*

☐ Yes ☐ No

1.2.3.2. If V1231=1: *How many children are homeschooled?*

_____

1.2.4. *How many are adults between 18 and 60?*

_____

1.2.5. *How many are over 60?*

_____

1.3. *Does anyone in your household have a personal computer?*

☐ Yes ☐ No

1.3.1. If V13=1: *Does the computer have Internet service?*

☐ Yes ☐ No

1.3.1.1. If V131=1: *Is your Internet service high speed, such as cable modem or DSL?*

☐ Yes ☐ No

1.4. *Is there anyone in your household whose primary language is not English?*

☐ Yes ☐ No

1.5. *Is anyone in your household employed as a teacher?*

☐ Yes ☐ No

1.6. *Are any of the members of your household visually challenged? (Prompt: Anyone who has such difficulty seeing that they need large-print, braille, or audio books?)*

☐ Yes ☐ No

Section 2

Now I am going to ask you about some specific _____ Library services. We want to know how much members of your household use these services. Please answer each question based on the total amount of each service used by you plus all the other members in your household combined. If you are not sure whether anyone uses the service, just answer "none" or "no."

> *Programming Note:* Randomize the order of the major groups of questions in Section 2. Also, build in consistency checks so that replacement purchase must be less than library usage.

STAFF1. *The _____ Library staff can answer questions, help people find information and materials, or suggest things to read. Staff also may help with homework, help people learning to read, or help those who have difficulty with English. During the past year, about how many hours did members of your household spend getting help from _____ Library staff?*

> _____ hours/year   [If "zero," go to next relevant block.]

> *Programming Note:* Convert hours/year to hours/month for storage in database.

STAFF2. *Your household can hire a local tutor to coach reading, help with homework, or teach English skills. How many hours of tutoring per month, if any, did members of your household pay to receive during the past year?*

> _____ hours/month

STAFF3. *There are research companies that can be reached by phone or e-mail from your home or workplace. For a fee, you can have these companies provide answers to questions or find information for you. They charge fees according to the amount of time it takes them to research your question. How many hours of research per month, if any, did members of your household purchase from such companies during the past year?*

> _____ hours/month

STAFF4. *Suppose that the _____ Library was closed indefinitely due to storm, fire, or earthquake damage and could not provide staff to help you. Also suppose that you can hire a local tutor to coach reading, help with homework, or teach English skills for **TUTORPR** per hour. Or, you can obtain information by phone or e-mail from a private research company for **STAFFPR** per research hour. How many (if any) of the **STAFF1** hours your household spends with _____ Library staff would you replace by hiring a local tutor for **TUTORPR** per hour?*

> _____ hours/year

STAFF5. *How many (if any) of the* <u>**STAFF1**</u> *hours your household spends with* _____ *Library staff would you replace by purchasing research services by phone or e-mail request for* <u>**STAFFPR**</u> *per research hour?*

_____ hours/year

MAG. *Does anyone in your household look at magazines from the* _____ *Library?*

☐ Yes ☐ No [If "no," skip all MAG and MAGF questions; go to next relevant block.]

MAG1. *About how many different magazines in English do people in your household look at from the* _____ *Library?*

_____ [If "zero" and V14=1, go to MAGF1; otherwise, if "zero" go to next relevant block.]

MAG2. *How many subscriptions to different magazines in English does your household pay to get per year?*

_____/year

MAG3. *Suppose that the* _____ *Library was closed indefinitely due to storm, fire, or earthquake damage and could not provide the magazines your household wants. Also suppose that each different magazine subscription costs* <u>**MAGPR**</u> *per year. How many (if any) of the* <u>**MAG1**</u> *magazines your household uses at the* _____ *Library would they pay to replace at* <u>**MAGPR**</u> *per subscription per year?*

_____/year

MAGF1. If V14=1: *About how many different magazines in languages other than English do members of your household look at from the* _____ *Library?*

_____ [If "zero," go to next relevant block.]

2MAGF2. If V14=1: *How many subscriptions to different magazines in languages other than English does your household pay to get per year?*

_____/year

2MAGF3. If V14=1: *Suppose that the* _____ *Library was closed indefinitely due to storm, fire, or earthquake damage and could not provide the magazines your household wants. Also suppose that each subscription to a magazine in a language other than English costs* <u>**MAGFPR**</u> *per year. How many (if any) of the* <u>**MAGF1**</u> *magazines your household uses at the* _____ *Library would they pay to replace at* <u>**MAGFPR**</u> *per subscription per year?*

_____/year

NEWS. *Does anyone in your household read newspapers from the* _____ *Library?*

☐ Yes ☐ No [If "no," skip all NEWS and NEWSF questions; go to next relevant block.]

NEWS1. *About how many copies of English-language newspapers do your household members read at the _____ Library? By copy we mean a specific edition of a specific paper, so count Monday's and Tuesday's edition of the same paper as two copies. Also, if someone reads two different papers on Monday, count each as a copy.*

      _____/week   [If "zero" and V14=1, go to NEWSF1; otherwise, if "zero" go to next relevant block.]

NEWS2. *How many copies of English-language newspapers does your household buy per week?*

      _____/week

NEWS3. *Suppose that the _____ Library was closed indefinitely due to storm, fire, or earthquake damage and could not provide the newspapers your household wants. Also suppose that each newspaper copy costs* <u>NEWSPR</u>. *How many (if any) of the* <u>NEWS1</u> *copies of newspapers your household uses at the _____ Library would your household replace by buying copies at* <u>NEWSPR</u> *each?*

      _____/week

NEWSF1. If V14=1: *About how many copies of newspapers in a language other than English do your household members use per week from the _____ Library? By copy we mean a specific edition of a specific paper, so count Monday's and Tuesday's edition of the same paper as two copies. Also, if someone reads two different papers on Monday, count each as a copy.* [If V14=0, then NEWSF1=0]

      _____/week   [If "zero," go to next relevant block.]

NEWSF2. If V14=1: *How many newspaper copies in a language other than English does your household buy per week?*

      _____/week

NEWSF3. If V14=1: *Suppose that the _____ Library was closed indefinitely due to storm, fire, or earthquake damage and could not provide the newspapers your household wants. Also suppose that each newspaper copy in a language other than English costs* <u>NEWSFPR</u>. *How many (if any) of the* <u>NEWSF1</u> *copies your household uses at the _____ Library would your household replace by buying copies at* <u>NEWSFPR</u> *each?*

      _____/week

BOOKS1. *About how many different books for adult readers do your household members borrow per month from the _____ Library?*

      _____/month   [If "zero," go to next relevant block.]

BOOKS2. *How many books does your household buy per month for its adult readers?*

      _____/month

BOOKS3. *Suppose that the _____ Library was closed indefinitely due to storm, fire, or earthquake damage and could not provide the books your adult readers want. Also suppose that paperback copies of similar books are available for your household to purchase at a price of BOOKPR each. How many (if any) of the BOOKS1 books your household borrows per month from the _____ Library would they replace by purchases at BOOKPR per book?*

_____/month

Programming Note: NOCMP1 through ENCYC should be treated as one block.

NOCOMP1. If V13=0: *People can use computers at the _____ Library for many different purposes: e-mailing friends and relatives, surfing the Internet, getting information about buying cars or other major purchases, tracking their stocks and investments, researching medical or legal information, learning to use computers and software, or doing their homework for school. About how many hours per week do your household members use computers at the _____ Library?*

_____ hours/week   [If the response is "none," follow up with "# per month?"]

_____ hours/month   [Convert and store response as hours/month. If "zero" or no response, go to ENCYC.]

NOCOMP2. If V13=0: *Suppose that the _____ Library was closed indefinitely due to storm, fire, or earthquake damage and could not meet your household's computing needs. You would have at least three options: rent, buy, or do without. If your household chooses to do without a computer, no one in your household will have e-mail, Internet, or any electronic information services. Many copy centers like Kinko's and Copy Max rent computer time for word processing, e-mail, and Internet service. Suppose that computer time costs COMPRENT per hour at a private vendor like Kinko's, or that you could buy a computer (excluding Internet service) for about COMPPR per month. Would you rent at COMPRENT/hour, buy a computer system at COMPPR per month, or do without computer services?*

☐ Don't know/can't answer   [Go to next relevant block.]

☐ Do without   [Go to ENCYC.]

☐ Buy   [Go to COMP2.]

☐ Rent   [Go to CMPCLS1.]

[Ask COMP1 if V13=1 and V1311=0. If V1311=1, then skip to CMPCLS1. Otherwise (e.g., V13=1 and V131=#N/A), go to next relevant block.]

COMP1. *Do any members of your household use _____ Library computers for high-speed Internet, software programs they don't have, or searching the _____ Library's electronic information sources? (If your household uses the computers only to search the library's own catalog, answer "no.")*

☐ Yes   ☐ No

Programming Note: If COMP1=0, go to ENCYC.

COMP2. *The _____ Library computers have high-speed Internet service. Suppose that the _____ Library was closed indefinitely due to storm, fire, or earthquake damage and could not meet your household's computing needs.*

If V131≠1: *Would your household install modem Internet service for **NETMODPR** per month, high-speed Internet service for **NETHSPR** per month, or do without Internet service?*

☐ Modem   ☐ High speed   ☐ Do without   [Go to CMPSFT.]

If V131=1: *Would your household upgrade to high-speed Internet service for an additional **NETHSPR** – **NETMODPR** per month?*

☐ Upgrade to high speed   ☐ No

CMPSFT. *The _____ Library computers have software for word processing, spreadsheets, and presentations. Suppose that the _____ Library was closed indefinitely due to storm, fire, or earthquake damage and could not meet your household's software needs. Would your household purchase a software suite such as Microsoft Office for **CMPSFTPR** per month?*

☐ Yes   ☐ No

CMPCLS1. *About how many hours per year do your household members spend at the _____ Library taking computer classes or getting tips from library staff on using computers?*

_____ hours/year   [If CMPCLS1=0 or #N/A, and if COMP2=modem or high speed, go to EREF1. If CMPCLS1=0 or #N/A, and if COMP2=do without, go to CDENCYC.]

CMPCLS2. *How many hours of computer classes, workshops, or tutorials did your household members pay to take last year?*

_____ hours/year

CMPCLS3. *Suppose that the _____ Library had been closed indefinitely due to storm, fire, or earthquake damage and could not provide computer classes. Also suppose that you could pay to take computer classes, workshops, or instruction for **CMPCLSPR** per hour per person. How many (if any) of the **CMPCLS1** hours of* *library computer instruction last year would your household have replaced with instruction elsewhere at **CMPCLSPR** per hour per person?*

_____ hours/year [If COMP2=do without, go to ENCYC.]

EREF1. *Today many library information sources are electronic. You can use them only with a computer. As I read the following list, please say "yes" if someone in your household uses that type of electronic information from the _____ Library. If no one does or you are uncertain, please say "no."*

EREF1.1. *Electronic copies of articles from major newspapers and magazines*

☐ Yes   ☐ No

EREF1.2. *Electronic scientific, professional, medical, or academic journals*

☐ Yes   ☐ No

EREF1.3. *Business and investment information, directories, publications, and data (such as Wall Street Journal, Value Line, Dun and Bradstreet)*

☐ Yes   ☐ No

EREF1.4. *Genealogy (searching family roots)*

☐ Yes   ☐ No

[If SUM(EREF11 . . . EREF14)=0 or ALL=#N/A, go to ENCYC.]

EREF2. *Suppose that _____ Library was closed indefinitely due to storm, fire, or earthquake damage and could not provide the information services your household wants. Your household could subscribe directly to replace electronic information services they currently use through the _____ Library. Answer "yes" if your household would subscribe. Otherwise, say "no."*

EREF2.1. IF EREF11=1: *An electronic subscription providing articles from major newspapers and magazines for **EPRDCLPR** per month (searchable; downloadable full-text such as ProQuest, ABI Inform, Article First, First Search, Reference USA)*

☐ Yes   ☐ No

EREF2.2. IF EREF12=1: *An electronic subscription providing scientific, professional, medical, or academic journals for **EJRNLPR** per month*

☐ Yes   ☐ No

EREF2.3. IF EREF13=1: *An electronic subscription providing business and investment directories, publications, and data for **EBSFNPR** per month (such as Standard and Poor's, Wall Street Journal, Dun and Bradstreet, Sorkins)*

☐ Yes   ☐ No

EREF2.4. IF EREF14=1: *An electronic subscription providing genealogy information, such as Ancestry.com, for __EGENPR__ per year*

☐ Yes   ☐ No

[Go to next relevant block.]

CDENCYC. *Suppose that the _____ Library was closed indefinitely due to storm, fire, or earthquake damage. Would your household buy an encyclopedia on CD or DVD, such as Microsoft's Encarta, at __EREFPR__?*

☐ Yes   ☐ No

Programming Note: Divide response by 5 for recording in the database.

[Go to next relevant block.]

ENCYC. *Suppose that the _____ Library was closed indefinitely due to storm, fire, or earthquake damage. Would your household buy a home reference collection, including an encyclopedia, dictionary, and atlas, at __ENCYCPR__?*

☐ Yes   ☐ No

Programming Note: Divide response by 5 for recording in the database.

[Go to next relevant block.]

[If V12=0, then CHLDBK1=0 and go to next relevant block. If V12=1, ask]

CHLDBK1. *About how many children's books do your household members borrow per month from the _____ Library?*

_____/month   [If CHLDBK1=0 or #N/A, go to next relevant block.]

CHLDBK2. If V12=1: *How many children's books does your household buy per month?*

_____/month

CHLDBK3. If V12=1: *Suppose that the _____ Library was closed indefinitely due to storm, fire, or earthquake damage and could not provide the children's books your household wants. Also suppose that paperback copies of similar children's books are available for your household to purchase at a price of __CHLDBKPR__ each. How many (if any) of the __CHLDBK1__ children's books your household borrows each month would you replace by buying books at __CHLDBKPR__ per book?*

_____/month

AV. *Does anyone in your household borrow CDs, audiotapes, books on tape or disk, DVDs, or videotapes from the _____ Library?*

☐ Yes   ☐ No   [If AV=0 or #N/A, skip all AV questions; go to next relevant block.]

AV1. *About how many different music CDs or tapes do your household members borrow per month from the _____ Library?*

_____/month   [If "zero," go to AV4.]

AV2. *How many music CDs or tapes do members of your household purchase per month?*

_____/month

AV3. *Suppose that the _____ Library was closed indefinitely due to storm, fire, or earthquake damage and could not provide the music CDs or tapes members of your household want. Also suppose that CDs and tapes cost* <u>AUDIOPR</u> *each in stores. How many (if any) of the* <u>AV1</u> *CDs and tapes your household borrows would you replace by buying them at* <u>AUDIOPR</u> *each?*

_____/month

AV4. *How many videotapes or DVDs do your household members borrow per month from the _____ Library?*

_____/month   [If AV4=0, go to AV7.]

AV5. *How many videotapes or DVDs does your household rent per month from Blockbuster, Hollywood Video, or other rental shops?*

_____/month

AV6. *Suppose that the _____ Library was closed indefinitely due to storm, fire, or earthquake damage and could not provide the videos your household wants. Also suppose that rentals from rental shops like Blockbuster or Hollywood Video cost* <u>VISUALPR</u> *each. How many (if any) of the* <u>AV4</u> *your household borrows per month would you replace by renting at* <u>VISUALPR</u> *each?*

_____/month

AV7. *About how many different books on tape or disk do your household members borrow per month from the _____ Library?*

_____/month   [If "zero," go to next relevant block.]

AV8. *How many books on tape or disk do members of your household purchase or rent per month?*

_____/month

AV9. *Suppose that the _____ Library was closed indefinitely due to storm, fire, or earthquake damage and could not provide the books on tape or disk members of your household want. Also suppose that books on tape or disk cost __BKTAPPR__ each to rent from stores. How many (if any) of the __AV7__ CDs and tapes your household borrows would you replace by renting them at __BKTAPPR__ each?*

> _____/month   [If V12=0, then CHLDBK1=0 and go to next relevant block.
> If V12=1, ask:]

CHLDPRG1. *About how many shows, storytelling programs, reading activities, plays, or other programs provided at the _____ Library do the children in your household attend per year? Consider each child separately, so three children seeing the same show would count as attending three times.*

> _____/year   [If CHLDPRG1=0 or #N/A, go to next relevant block.]

CHLDPRG2. If V12=1: *How many tickets to similar plays, programs, and shows for children does your household purchase each year?*

> _____/year

CHLDPRG3. If V12=1: *Suppose that _____ Library was closed indefinitely due to storm, fire, or earthquake damage and could not provide children's programs. Also suppose that a ticket to a child's play, program, or show elsewhere costs __CHPRGPR__. How many (if any) of the __CHLDPRG1__ programs children in your household attended at the _____ Library would you replace by purchasing tickets at __CHPRGPR__ each?*

> _____/year

PROG1. *About how many special events such as performances, author visits, recitals, lectures, and other programs provided by the _____ Library do your adult household members attend per year? Consider each adult separately, so two adults seeing the same show would count as two attendances.*

> _____/year   [If PROG1=0 or #N/A, go to next relevant block.]

PROG2. *How many tickets do your adult household members purchase per year to attend similar programs and events?*

> _____/year

PROG3. *Suppose that the _____ Library was closed indefinitely due to storm, fire, or earthquake damage and could not provide programs. Also suppose that attending performances, author visits, recitals, and lectures cost __PROGPR__ per person elsewhere. How many (if any) of the __PROG1__ programs at the _____ Library would your household replace by purchasing additional tickets to events elsewhere at __PROGPR__ each?*

> _____/year

Section 3

If SPEND1=0, go to SECTION 4.

3.1. *My computer has totaled the amounts you said your household would spend to replace _____ Library services by buying additional books or magazines or other services. Based on your responses, your household would spend $**SPEND1** per year on additional purchases if these items or services were not available through the _____ Library. Suppose that all local taxes and fees to support the _____ Library were suspended during its closure. Is $**SPEND1** per year an amount your household could afford and would actually spend to replace _____ Library services?*

    ☐ Yes   ☐ No

    Programming Note: Formula should calculate extra spending, not consumer surplus.

[If V31=1, then V32=SPEND1 and go to Section 4. If V31=0, say:]

3.2. *Instead of $**SPEND1** per year, how much would your household spend per year for additional books, magazines, and other items to replace the materials and services you currently use from the _____ Library?*

    _____/year

First, I will read a list of _____ Library services. Then I will read each service category again and ask you the following question: In reducing the amount your household would spend to replace _____ Library services, would you spend less in that category?

Here are the categories of _____ Library services and the amount you said your household would spend to replace that service.

[Interviewer: read list of services and spending for each.]

In reducing the amount your household would spend to replace _____ Library services, would you spend less to replace

3.2.1. [If STAFFEX>0] *Help provided by library staff?*	$STAFFEX	☐ Yes ☐ No
3.2.2. [If MAGNEWEX>0] *Magazines and newspapers?*	$MAGNEWEX	☐ Yes ☐ No
3.2.3. [If CHILDEX>0] *Children's books and programs?*	$CHILDEX	☐ Yes ☐ No
3.2.4. [If ADULTEX>0] *Books and programs for adults?*	$ADULTEX	☐ Yes ☐ No
3.2.5. [If AVEX>0] *CDs, DVDs, and tapes?*	$AVEX	☐ Yes ☐ No
3.2.6. [If COMPUTEX>0] *Library computer usage and classes?*	$COMPUTEX	☐ Yes ☐ No

3.2.7. [If ELECTEX>0] *Electronic information services?* $\underline{\text{ELECTEX}}$ ☐ Yes ☐ No

3.2.8. [If ENCYCEX>0] *Encyclopedia?* $\underline{\text{ENCYCEX}}$ ☐ Yes ☐ No

Section 4

We have been discussing how your household uses the _____ Library. This next question is very important.

Suppose that the _____ Library and all its branches, buildings, books, and equipment are destroyed in an uninsurable disaster. Nothing from the library can be recovered, but no people or other buildings in your community are harmed—only the _____ Library is destroyed. A vote will be held to establish the appropriate type and amount of local taxes to restore the _____ Library and all its services just as they were before the disaster. If the vote fails, the _____ Library will no longer exist. Neither your household nor other members of your community will have access to any _____ Library services.

4.0. *What is the maximum amount of annual local taxes and fees you would vote for your household to pay to restore and maintain _____ Library services? Please round your estimate to the nearest $100. Should I repeat the question? Please take your time.*

$_____/year

4.0.1. [If 40=0 or "don't know" or "can't answer," then show screen:] *Please help us to understand why you don't know or can't answer.*

[Text field] _____

_____

4.0.2. [If V40<V32] *You stated earlier that you were willing to spend $\underline{\text{V32}}$ per year to replace _____ Library services if the library were closed indefinitely, yet you would be willing to pay only $\underline{\text{V40}}$ per year in taxes and fees to restore and maintain _____ Library services. Please help us to understand why these answers differ.*

[Text field] _____

_____

4.1. Alternative wording for question 4.0: *Now suppose a referendum is held to revise local taxes to restore and maintain the _____ Library so that it can again provide the same services you have today. If the referendum passes, your household would be required to pay $\underline{\text{TAX}}$ in taxes and fees each year for the _____ Library. If the referendum fails, there would be no _____ Library. Would you vote for or against the proposition?*

☐ For   ☐ Against   ☐ Don't know/can't answer

4.2. *Suppose the referendum had a different amount that your household would be required to pay. Suppose your household would be required to pay $TAX1 in taxes and fees each year to support the _____ Library if the referendum were to pass. Would you vote for or against the proposition?*

☐ For ☐ Against ☐ Don't know/can't answer

Please help us to understand your answer.

[Text field] _____

_____

Section 5

We are close to finishing. You have been very helpful. We have only a few more short questions for statistical purposes only. Remember that our research institute is legally bound to confidentiality. Once all interviews are completed, all names, street addresses, and phone numbers will be purged from the interview database.

5.0. *Which of the following categories best describes your age?* [Read categories and record response.]

☐ *18–25* ☐ *26–35* ☐ *36–45* ☐ *46–55* ☐ *56–65* ☐ *66–75* ☐ *over 75*

5.1. *What is the highest level of school that you completed?* [Read categories and record response.]

☐ *Some high school*

☐ *High school diploma or equivalent*

☐ *Some college/technical school or associate's degree*

☐ *Bachelor's degree*

☐ *Advanced degree beyond bachelor's level*

5.2. [If did not answer 5.1, skip 5.2 and go to 5.3. Otherwise, ask:] *What is the highest level of school completed by your spouse or partner?* [Read categories and record response.]

☐ *Some high school*

☐ *High school diploma or equivalent*

☐ *Some college/technical school or associate's degree*

☐ *Bachelor's degree*

☐ *Advanced degree beyond bachelor's level*

☐ *Don't know or not applicable*

5.3. *How would you describe your race or ethnic background?* [Do not read list.]

☐ African American/Black

☐ Caucasian/White

☐ American Indian

□ Asian

□ Hispanic/Chicano

□ Other

5.4. *Does your household rent or own your home?*

□ Rent   □ Own

5.5. *Which of the following categories best describes your household's before-tax income?* [Read categories and record response.]

□ *Less than 10 thousand dollars*

□ *Between 10 and 15 thousand*

□ *Between 15 and 20 thousand*

□ *Between 20 and 30 thousand*

□ *Between 30 and 40 thousand*

□ *Between 40 and 50 thousand*

□ *Between 50 and 60 thousand*

□ *Between 60 and 70 thousand*

□ *Between 70 and 85 thousand*

□ *Between 85 and 100 thousand*

[If any of these categories is checked, go to 5.6.]

□ *Over $100,000*

Because this project requires a fairly precise estimate of your household income to appropriately apply certain statistical models, would you please specify the amount to the nearest $20,000?

$_____

[Interviewer: If respondent refuses, then prompt: *I assure you that we are required to keep this information confidential.* If he or she still refuses, say *I understand.* Then go to 5.6.]

5.6. [Record the respondent's gender based on voice and dialogue. Ask only if uncertain.]

□ Male   □ Female

5.7. *Is there anything else you would like to say to the Library Director regarding the _____ Library?*

[If "no," leave blank; if "yes," record verbatim.]

6.0. [If V15=0, then say:] *That concludes the survey. Thank you for your time and cooperation. Your responses will help your library serve the community well.*

[If V15=1, say:] *May I please talk very briefly to the teacher in your household? I promise to take only a minute.* [Interviewer: If not available, go to 7.0.]

Do you use the _____ Library to help you with your work as a teacher?

☐ Yes   ☐ No   [If V60=0, go to 7.0.]

6.1. *Suppose that a natural disaster caused the _____ Library and all its branches and services to close indefinitely. I will read a list of _____ Library services. Consider whether the service is essential to maintaining the quality of your teaching. After each, say "yes" if it is a library service that you or your school would have to pay to replace. Otherwise, say "no."*

[Check all that apply.]

6.1.1. *Staff help*   ☐ Yes   ☐ No

6.1.2. *Magazines and newspapers*   ☐ Yes   ☐ No

6.1.3. *Children's books and programs*   ☐ Yes   ☐ No

6.1.4. *Books and programs for adults*   ☐ Yes   ☐ No

6.1.5. *CDs, DVDs, and tapes*   ☐ Yes   ☐ No

6.1.6. *Library computers or computer classes* ☐ Yes   ☐ No

6.1.7. *Electronic information sources*   ☐ Yes   ☐ No

6.1.8. *Encyclopedias*   ☐ Yes   ☐ No

6.2. *How much more would you or your school have to spend per year to maintain the quality of your teaching if the _____ Library were closed indefinitely?*

$_____/year   ☐ Don't know/can't answer

7.0. *That concludes the survey. Thank you for your time and cooperation. Your responses will help your library serve the community well.*

BUSINESS SURVEY INSTRUMENT

Hello, my name is _____. *I am calling on behalf of* _____, *Director of the* _____ *Public Library. May I please speak to* <u>*business patron's name*</u>*?* [If not available, record date and time of call and proceed to the next prospective respondent.]

We are conducting a survey of people who use the _____ *Library. I assure you this is a confidential survey. Your responses will help us understand how you use library services and how to serve you better. May I take a few minutes now to ask you some questions?*

◾ If "Yes," start the interview.

◾ If "No," ask: *May I call you later at a more convenient time?*

   • If "No," say: *Thank you for your time, good-bye.*

   • If "Yes," ask: *What time would be convenient?* (Record day and time _____ for follow-up.)

Do you use the _____ *Public Library for business or professional reasons?*

   ☐ No   [Thank respondent and terminate interview.]

   ☐ Yes   [Say:] *Today we are interested in speaking to you about using the library for business or professional purposes only.*

I am going to ask you about some specific public library services. Please answer each question as best you can. Indicate which services, if any, you use for business or professional purposes.

1. *Do you use business and phone directories from the library?*

   ☐ No or Don't Know (DK)   [GO TO 8]

   ☐ Yes   [Ask:]

2–4. *What are the three most important directories or reference sources you use? Please give the actual titles if you can.*

[Record the top three (unaided). But if the respondent says "don't know," "not sure," "can't remember," or something similar and cannot offer at least one reference source, prompt with: *Some examples include Dun's Regional Business Directory, Chamber of Commerce rosters, and the Directory of Corporate Affiliations.*]

2. _____ [GO TO 3]   ☐ DK/NA   [GO TO 8]

3. _____ [GO TO 4]   ☐ DK/NA   [GO TO 5]

4. _____ [GO TO 5]   ☐ DK/NA   [GO TO 5]

5–7. *If public libraries did not exist, would you either purchase or subscribe to or request that your firm purchase or subscribe to*

5. _____ ☐ Yes ☐ No ☐ DK/NA [Read open-end response from 2]

6. _____ ☐ Yes ☐ No ☐ DK/NA [Read open-end response from 3, if applicable]

7. _____ ☐ Yes ☐ No ☐ DK/NA [Read open-end response from 4, if applicable]

8. *Do you use library sources to access annual or corporate reports?*

☐ No [GO TO 15]

☐ Yes [Ask:]

9–11. *What are the three most important information sources you use? Please give the actual titles if you can.*

[Record the top three (unaided). But if the respondent says "don't know," "not sure," "can't remember," or something similar and cannot offer at least one reference source, prompt with: *Some examples include Standard and Poors, 10K reports, and Predicasts F&S.*]

9. _____ [GO TO 10] ☐ DK/NA [GO TO 15]

10. _____ [GO TO 11] ☐ DK/NA [GO TO 12]

11. _____ [GO TO 12] ☐ DK/NA [GO TO 12]

12–14. *If public libraries did not exist, would you either purchase or subscribe to or request that your firm purchase or subscribe to*

12. _____ ☐ Yes ☐ No ☐ DK/NA [Read open-end response from 9]

13. _____ ☐ Yes ☐ No ☐ DK/NA [Read open-end response from 10, if applicable]

14. _____ ☐ Yes ☐ No ☐ DK/NA [Read open-end response from 11, if applicable]

15. *Do you use library sources to access government data?*

☐ No [GO TO 22]

☐ Yes [Ask:]

16–18. *What are the three most important information sources you use for this purpose? Please give the actual titles if you can.*

[Record the top three (unaided). But if the respondent says "don't know," "not sure," "can't remember," or something similar and cannot offer at least one reference source, prompt with: *Some examples include Census of the Population, County Business Patterns, Statistical Abstracts of the U.S., and U.S. Patent.*]

16. _____   [GO TO 17] ☐ DK/NA [GO TO 22]

17. _____   [GO TO 18] ☐ DK/NA [GO TO 19]

18. _____   [GO TO 19] ☐ DK/NA [GO TO 19]

19–21. *If public libraries did not exist, would you either purchase or subscribe to or request that your firm purchase or subscribe to*

19. _____   ☐ Yes ☐ No ☐ DK/NA [Read open-end response from 16]

20. _____   ☐ Yes ☐ No ☐ DK/NA [Read open-end response from 17, if applicable]

21. _____   ☐ Yes ☐ No ☐ DK/NA [Read open-end response from 18, if applicable]

22. *Do you use library sources to access marketing/product data?*

☐ No   [GO TO 29]

☐ Yes   [Ask:]

23–25. *What are the three most important information sources you use for this purpose? Please give the actual titles if you can.*

[Record the top three (unaided). But if the respondent says "don't know," "not sure," "can't remember," or something similar and cannot offer at least one reference source, prompt with: *Some examples include Thomas' Register, Ward's Automotive Report, Advertiser's Red Book, and Rand McNally Commercial Atlas and Marketing Guide.*]

23. _____   [GO TO 24] ☐ DK/NA [GO TO 29]

24. _____   [GO TO 25] ☐ DK/NA [GO TO 26]

25. _____   [GO TO 26] ☐ DK/NA [GO TO 26]

26–28. *If public libraries did not exist, would you either purchase or subscribe to or request that your firm purchase or subscribe to*

26. _____   ☐ Yes ☐ No ☐ DK/NA [Read open-end response from 23]

27. _____   ☐ Yes   ☐ No   ☐ DK/NA   [Read open-end response from 24, if applicable]

28. _____   ☐ Yes   ☐ No   ☐ DK/NA   [Read open-end response from 25, if applicable]

29. **Do you use library sources to access tax references?**

      ☐ No   [GO TO 36]

      ☐ Yes   [Ask:]

30–32. **What are the three most important references you use for this purpose? Please give the actual titles if you can.**

[Record the top three (unaided). But if the respondent says "don't know," "not sure," "can't remember," or something similar and cannot offer at least one reference source, prompt with: **Some examples include Commerce Clearing House U.S. Tax Cases and Commerce Clearing House Tax Court Decisions.**]

30. _____   [GO TO 31]   ☐ DK/NA   [GO TO 36]

31. _____   [GO TO 32]   ☐ DK/NA   [GO TO 33]

32. _____   [GO TO 33]   ☐ DK/NA   [GO TO 33]

33–35. **If public libraries did not exist, would you either purchase or subscribe to or request that your firm purchase or subscribe to**

33. _____   ☐ Yes   ☐ No   ☐ DK/NA   [Read open-end response from 30]

34. _____   ☐ Yes   ☐ No   ☐ DK/NA   [Read open-end response from 31, if applicable]

35. _____   ☐ Yes   ☐ No   ☐ DK/NA   [Read open-end response from 32, if applicable]

36. **Do you use library sources to access financial/investment data for business and professional purposes?**

      ☐ No   [GO TO 43]

      ☐ Yes   [Ask:]

37–39. **What are the three most important information sources you use for this purpose? Please give the actual titles if you can.**

[Record the top three (unaided). But if the respondent says "don't know," "not sure," "can't remember," or something similar and cannot offer at least one reference source, prompt with: **Some examples include Dun and Bradstreet, Valueline, Standard and Poors, and the Thompson/Polk Bank Directory.**]

37. _____   [GO TO 38]   ☐ DK/NA   [GO TO 43]

38. _____ [GO TO 39] ☐ DK/NA [GO TO 40]

39. _____ [GO TO 40] ☐ DK/NA [GO TO 40]

40–42. *If public libraries did not exist, would you either purchase or subscribe to or request that your firm purchase or subscribe to*

40. _____ ☐ Yes ☐ No ☐ DK/NA [Read open-end response from 37]

41. _____ ☐ Yes ☐ No ☐ DK/NA [Read open-end response from 38, if applicable]

42. _____ ☐ Yes ☐ No ☐ DK/NA [Read open-end response from 39, if applicable]

43. *Do you use films, videotapes, or sets of videotapes for business/professional purposes from the library?*

      ☐ No [GO TO 51]

      ☐ Yes [Ask:]

44. *Do you or does your firm purchase films, videotapes, or sets of videotapes for your business/professional use?*

      ☐ Yes ☐ No

45–47. *What are the three most important videotapes, tape sets, or films you borrow from the library? Please give the actual titles if you can.*

[Record the top three (unaided)—no prompts]

45. _____ [GO TO 46] ☐ DK/NA [GO TO 51]

46. _____ [GO TO 47] ☐ DK/NA [GO TO 48]

47. _____ [GO TO 48] ☐ DK/NA [GO TO 48]

48. *If public libraries did not exist, how many additional tapes or films like _____ would you or your firm purchase per year?* [Read open-end response from 45]

      _____ ☐ DK/NA

49. *If public libraries did not exist, how many additional tapes or films like _____ would you or your firm purchase per year?* [Read open-end response from 46 if applicable]

      _____ ☐ DK/NA

50. *If public libraries did not exist, how many additional tapes or films like* _____ *would you or your firm purchase per year?* [Read open-end response from 47 if applicable]

　　　_____　□ DK/NA

51. *Do you use the library to access other reference materials?*

　　　□ No　[GO TO 58]

　　　□ Yes　[Ask:]

52–54. *What are the three most important of these other reference materials you use? Please give the actual titles if you can.*

[Record the top three (unaided). But if the respondent says "don't know," "not sure," "can't remember," or something similar and cannot offer at least one reference source, prompt with: *Some examples include Black's Law Dictionary, Labor Relations Reference Manual, Hoover's Handbook of American Business, and the Wall Street Journal Index.*]

52. _____　[GO TO 53]　□ DK/NA　[GO TO 58]

53. _____　[GO TO 54]　□ DK/NA　[GO TO 55]

54. _____　[GO TO 55]　□ DK/NA　[GO TO 55]

55–57. *If public libraries did not exist, would you either purchase or subscribe to or request that your firm purchase or subscribe to*

55. _____　□ Yes　□ No　□ DK/NA　[Read open-end response from 52]

56. _____　□ Yes　□ No　□ DK/NA　[Read open-end response from 53, if applicable]

57. _____　□ Yes　□ No　□ DK/NA　[Read open-end response from 54, if applicable]

58. *Do you use the library for computer training services related to your business/ profession?*

　　　□ No　[GO TO 61]

　　　□ Yes

59. *Typically, about how many hours per month do you use computers at the library for activities such as word processing, creating presentation materials, spreadsheets, or Internet access?*

　　　_____ hours/month

60. *If public libraries did not exist, would you pay or request that your firm pay to get computer training services?*

    ☐ Yes ☐ No ☐ DK/NA

Just as a reminder, your answers should be based on the public library services you use for business or professional purposes only.

61. *Do you use the library to access business periodicals or newspapers?*

    ☐ No [GO TO 68]

    ☐ Yes [Ask:]

62–64. *What are the three most important periodicals or newspapers you use?*

[Record the top three (unaided). But if the respondent says "don't know," "not sure," "can't emem ber," or something similar and cannot offer at least one reference source, prompt with: *Some examples include Business Week, Fortune, Wall Street Journal, and New York Times.*]

62. _____ [GO TO 63] ☐ DK/NA [GO TO 68]

63. _____ [GO TO 64] ☐ DK/NA [GO TO 65]

64. _____ [GO TO 65] ☐ DK/NA [GO TO 65]

65–67. *If public libraries did not exist, would you either subscribe to or request that your firm subscribe to*

65. _____ ☐ Yes ☐ No ☐ DK/NA [Read open-end response from 62]

66. _____ ☐ Yes ☐ No ☐ DK/NA [Read open-end response from 63, if applicable]

67. _____ ☐ Yes ☐ No ☐ DK/NA [Read open-end response from 64, if applicable]

68. *Do you get research help or informational assistance from the library staff?*

    ☐ No [GO TO 75]

    ☐ Yes [Ask:]

69–71. *What are the three most important types of help or assistance you receive?*

[Record the top three (unaided)—no prompts]

69. _____ [GO TO 70] ☐ DK/NA [GO TO 75]

70. _____ [GO TO 71] ☐ DK/NA [GO TO 72]

71. _____ [GO TO 72] ☐ DK/NA [GO TO 72]

72. *If public libraries did not exist, how many hours of information brokerage services would you or your firm purchase per year to (help) _____?* [Read open-end response from 69]

      _____   ☐ DK/NA

73. *If public libraries did not exist, how many hours of information brokerage services would you or your firm purchase per year to (help) _____?* [Read open-end response from 70]

      _____   ☐ DK/NA

74. *If public libraries did not exist, how many hours of information brokerage services would you or your firm purchase per year to (help) _____?* [Read open-end response from 71]

      _____   ☐ DK/NA

75. *What other library service (if any) is important to your firm that was not already mentioned?*

      _____ [GO TO 76]

      ☐ None   [GO TO 79]

76. *If public libraries did not exist, would your firm pay to get _____?*

      ☐ Yes   ☐ No   ☐ DK/NA [Read open-end response from 75]

77. *What other library service is important to your firm besides the one you just mentioned?*

      _____ [GO TO 78]

      ☐ None   [GO TO 79]

78. *If public libraries did not exist, would your firm pay to get _____?*

      ☐ Yes   ☐ No   ☐ DK/NA   [Read open-end response from 77]

79. *About how many employees work at your regional location?* [Read categories]

      ☐ *Fewer than 6*   ☐ *Between 6 and 20*   ☐ *Between 20 and 100*

      ☐ *More than 100*

80. *About how many employees work for your entire company?* [Read categories]

      ☐ *Fewer than 6*   ☐ *Between 6 and 100*   ☐ *Between 100 and 1,000*

      ☐ *More than 1,000*

81. *If further clarification is needed for any of the responses I entered, may we call you back?*

      ☐ Yes   ☐ No   ☐ DK/NA

82. [Record the respondent's gender based on voice and dialogue. Ask only if uncertain.]

☐ Male   ☐ Female   ☐ DK/Refused

83. *Finally, is there anything else you would like to say to the Library Director regarding the public library?*

[If no, leave blank; if yes, record verbatim.]

That concludes the survey. As promised, you get free [GIFT] as a token of appreciation. [If applicable, read gift options from the list and record the selection.]

Thank you for your time and cooperation.

Calculating and Reporting Survey Response Rates

KNOWLEDGEABLE READERS OF SURVEY RESEARCH ARE OFTEN SKEPTICS. They know that unscrupulous researchers sometimes manipulate survey instruments and results to generate whatever skewed answers they wish.

To assure readers and build credibility, early in the study's report a wise author will offer some basic information about how the surveys were conducted. A short section and associated appendix reporting how respondents were selected (sampled), how many responded (sample size), response rates, and any checks or corrections for response bias help assure potential critics that the study and its conclusions are credible. This appendix illustrates how to calculate response rates, report sample size, and conduct bias checks in library CBA studies.

RESPONSE RATES

Think of a response rate as a success rate. In some ways, the response rate for a survey is similar to a batting average in baseball. A player's batting average is a percentage that reflects the number of successful hits given the number of times the batter has been at the plate. The goal of the sample surveys is to contact a number of active, representative library users to collect information about how they use and value their library and its services. The response rate to the survey reflects the percentage of the library users in the sample whom researchers succeeded in reaching and interviewing.

We use the information from the sample of respondents to draw inferences about the use of the library by all library users (i.e., the population of library users). Given a scientifically selected sample taken from the population of library users, if more library users in the sample respond to the survey, the survey's response rate is higher. A higher response rate gives readers greater confidence that the respondents are representative of the library's users. The more representative the respondents, the more credible the study's inferences about the population of library users, especially how they use and value their library and its services.

Adjusting the Library's Count of Eligible Users

We begin by adjusting the library's population count of active cardholding households (the filtered database) using information from the survey. The survey process provides additional information about the validity of the records in the filtered database provided by the library's IT staff.

If the library's cardholder database is well maintained, then cardholder records should be complete and up-to-date with respect to activity, addresses, and telephone contacts. Interviewers rarely should encounter incomplete, disconnected, or inaccurate telephone numbers. Households who respond should affirm that one or more members of the household have library cards and have used the library during the previous twelve months.

Researchers can compute an error rate based on the percentage of households contacted who offer responses suggesting that they are ineligible to participate in the survey. Researchers then reduce the library's count of active cardholding households proportionally.

For example, figure D.1 illustrates data for a hypothetical survey of cardholding households.

Section C.2 reports the number of ineligible responses: 34 households stated that they had not used the library during the past twelve months; 26 were ineligible for other reasons. Thus, 60 records in the sample were inactive or ineligible.

In section C.1 of the figure, note that 551 respondents completed the survey via the Internet. In addition, 539 cardholding households who had not completed the survey by Web responded later via follow-up telephone interviews. According to section C.4, another 9 households completed only part of the Web survey but enough to indicate clearly that they were active and eligible. Thus, 60 of 1,159 records were inactive or ineligible—an error rate of 5.2 percent (line D1).

As reported in section A of the figure, the library's IT staff produced a filtered database of 26,841 active cardholding households as the population of library users. Because 5.2 percent of the households contacted were ineligible to participate in the survey, researchers reduced the library's count of the active cardholding population of library users by 5.2 percent to an adjusted population of 25,451 cardholding households.

Please remember that an accurate count of active cardholding households is critical to the estimation of library benefits for general users. Researchers multiply the sample estimate of library benefits per household by the population count of active cardholding households to estimate total library benefits for all households using the library.

To some, the adjustment we outline above may not be sufficiently conservative. In our illustration, we assume that records with undeliverable invitations or wrong or disconnected phone numbers have an ineligibility rate no greater than the households who responded to the survey. We have no reason to believe otherwise. After all, library records indicate that these households used library services during the past year, just as responding households did. Households whose invitations were returned may merely have moved elsewhere, perhaps even in the library district. Households whose invitations were delivered, but whose phone numbers were wrong or disconnected, may still live in the library's district and continue to use library services. They may have discontinued landline telephone service for financial reasons or have switched to cellular phone service.

A. Population of active households after filtering:		26,841
A1. Net population of active households:		25,451
B. Sample		
B1. Original sample size:		2,501
Records not used	0	
B2. Net sample size		2,501
C. Disposition of sample		
C1. Total completions		1,090
Completions	539	
Web completions	551	
C2. Not active or ineligible		60
Stated no card use by household in last 12 months	34	
Not eligible	26	
C3. Disconnected or wrong number		255
Line disconnected	161	
Wrong number	94	
C4. Nonresponse		1,096
Partial web completion	9	
Foreign language	30	
No answer	495	
Only juvenile at home	7	
"Do not call" ("decline")	8	
Refused	436	
"Return mail"	111	
C5. Net sample size		2,501
D1. Error rate (Ineligible divided by total records responding)		5.2%
D2. Projected no-answer records ineligible*		69
D3. Net sample size after adjusting for inactive and ineligible records		2,372
D4. Response rate		46%
D5. Estimated active valid households in population		25,451

*Calculated as: (Records that could be ineligible) × (Error rate)

FIGURE D.1
Calculating the survey response rate

Even so, you or members of your research team may believe that households whose records are inaccurate or incomplete should be eliminated from the count of active cardholding households. If so, you can reduce the size of the population and sample more severely and generate results even more conservative than those we prescribe.

Calculating and Reporting
the Response Rate

The response rate for the survey, expressed as a percentage, is based on the number of complete responses divided by the sample size adjusted for ineligible records. Figure D.1 illustrates the calculation of a response rate.

Numerator: Number of Completions

According to line C.1 of figure D.1, 1,090 households completed the survey by Web or phone. The numerator of the response rate calculation is 1,090.

Denominator: Adjusted Sample Size

From the library's filtered database of 26,841 records, the IT staff followed researchers' instruction to draw a stratified random sample of 2,501 households to whom the director sent letters of invitation to participate in the survey. Next we reduce the size of the sample to obtain the denominator for the response rate calculation. To make the adjustment, we must estimate the number of records in the sample that are ineligible.

In section C.3, we see that 255 records contained wrong or disconnected phone numbers. Interviewers could not reach other households in the sample due to invalid addresses or telephone numbers. Automated messages indicated that 161 phone lines had been disconnected, and 94 calls resulted in wrong numbers.

According to section C.4, an additional 1,096 households did not complete the survey for a variety of other reasons: 9 began the Web survey but did not complete it or a follow-up telephone interview; 30 households spoke in a language other than English or Spanish; 7 calls reached only a juvenile at the residence; 495 did not complete the Web survey or answer any of the repeated calls by the interviewers; 436 did not respond by Web and then declined an interviewer's phone request; 8 households contacted the library to decline the invitation to participate; 111 invitations were returned by the postal service as undeliverable.

With the exception of the 9 partial completions, the remaining 1,342 records of the original sample described in the preceding two paragraphs may or may not be eligible. We assume that the error rate for these records is the same as the 5.2 percent error rate for the records for which we were able to check eligibility. Thus, 69 of the 1,222 records are likely to have been ineligible. Adding these 69 records deemed likely to be ineligible to the 60 records known to be ineligible yields a total of 129 ineligible records. Deducting these 129 records from the original sample of 2,501 yields an adjusted sample size of 2,372. Alternatively, one can get the same answer by multiplying the sample size of 2,501 by the eligibility rate of $[1 - 0.052]$.

Response Rate Calculation

The percent response rate is the quotient of the number of completed surveys divided by the adjusted sample size. In the example, the number of completions is 1,090. The adjusted sample size is 2,372. The response rate (line D.4) is 46 percent.

TESTS AND CORRECTIONS FOR RESPONSE BIAS

In appendix B, we suggest that you examine your library's cardholder database to see what information it contains about library users. We recommend that you select a few of these characteristics to develop stratified random samples for surveys in your study. To see if the completed responses are representative of the original sample and population, test the distribution of characteristics of the respondents who completed the survey to see if it is significantly different from the distribution of characteristics of the original sample and population.

Chi-Square Test for Response Bias

One simple statistical test is a chi-square contingency table. The table arrays the numbers of library users by the characteristics selected by the researchers. Imagine creating such a table for the original population and another table for the respondents completing the survey. If the respondents are representative of the original population, then, in percentage terms, the two distributions should be very similar. The chi-square test merely checks to see if the frequency distributions are sufficiently dissimilar to invalidate the presumption that the completed surveys are representative of the population.

To illustrate this test, consider a library that has stratified its user population by amount of library use. This is an important consideration in estimating benefits in a CBA study. Those who use the library more often may value library services more than other cardholders and hence be more likely to invest their time in responding to a survey about the library. If those responding to the survey tend to be those who value the library more, then survey responses may disproportionately represent the library's biggest cheerleaders rather than the population of library users as a whole. Such a bias would inflate the results of the study.

Also suppose that the library has used the combined Web and telephone modes of survey recommended here. Then whether or not the household uses e-mail could influence the household's likelihood of responding to the survey. Computer literacy and access to a computer might also influence the household's valuation of library services. Assume that this library's staff has aggressively sought to add cardholder e-mail addresses to the records of its cardholder database. For these reasons, the library also stratifies its sample by whether or not the library record includes an e-mail address.

Table D.1 illustrates the information for this library. Recall that each household is identified by a corresponding library card record. If an adult and juvenile(s) in the household have library cards, the selection process retains the adult's library card record.

In table D.1, the column heads identify the strata for the sampling. For example, the first stratum identifies households that have used the corresponding library card 45 times or less since its creation and the card record has no e-mail address; the fourth stratum identifies households that have used the corresponding library card more than 45 times since its creation and the card record contains an e-mail address. The last column gives totals by row.

The first row of the table distributes responding households across the survey strata. For example, 127 households completing the survey had used the corresponding library card 45 times or less and had no e-mail address on the record; 507 households completed the survey.

TABLE D.1
Chi-square test for response bias

	USE 1–45 W/O E-MAIL	USE 1–45 W/ E-MAIL	USE > 46 W/O E-MAIL	USE > 46 W/ E-MAIL	TOTAL
Completions	127	52	258	70	507
Expected	167.17	85.04	205.09	49.70	507
Population	4,484	2,281	5,501	1,333	13,599
Chi-squared	9.65	12.84	13.65	8.29	44.44
Weights	1.32	1.64	0.79	0.71	

Notes: Critical value (df = 3,.05) = 7.185 => response bias. Strata are based on "use" and whether or not there is an e-mail address in the record. The sample of households completing the survey is biased toward heavy users.

The third row of the table distributes the filtered population of households across the survey strata. For example, 4,484 of the 13,599 households had used the corresponding library card 45 times or less since its creation and their card records had no e-mail address.

The second row of the spreadsheet calculates expected sample frequencies based on the population distribution of characteristics. For example, consider the figure of 167.17 in the first cell of the row. Given that 4,484 of the 13,599 households (about 33 percent) have used their corresponding library card 45 times or less since its creation and have no e-mail address, one would expect about 33 percent of the 507 households in the sample (i.e., about 167 households) to have the same characteristics. Thus, if the sample of completed interviews is representative of the population, about 167 households in the sample of completed interviews should have used the corresponding library card 45 times or less since its creation and have no e-mail address in their library record.

For table D.1, the chi-square statistic for the contingency table is 44.44. This exceeds a critical value of 7.185 (degrees of freedom = 3, alpha = .05). Thus, the researchers must reject the null hypothesis that the sample of households completing the survey is representative of the population with respect to the joint characteristics of usage and electronic access. Chi-square contingency table analysis is a common topic in most college statistics texts.

To gain a better sense of the nature of the response bias, examine the expected frequencies (second row) versus the actual completion frequencies (first row). It is apparent that households that use the library more were more likely to complete the survey than households that use the library less. This is consistent with our concerns that led us to stratify the sample according to library use. Now that we know the sample of completed interviews is biased, possibly in a way that might distort our benefit projections, we should attempt to correct our analysis for the bias.

Weighting Responses to Correct for Response Bias

One way to adjust for response bias in the sample of completed interviews is to weight the data. Using weighted data to calculate such important results as benefits per household ensures that underrepresented segments of the population receive appropriate consideration and that overrepresented segments receive less. Most statistical packages offer the option of applying weights to analysis of data.

Table D.1 illustrates the calculation of weights to correct for response bias. For example, in the Weights row, the weight for the first column is 1.32. This weight is calculated as the ratio of the expected sample frequency for the stratum (167) to the actual sample frequency (127). This weight applies to sample observations for households with low use and no e-mail address. These households were underrepresented in the sample of completed interviews. Using a weight exceeding 1.0 gives these observations greater weight in the calculation of sample statistics.

In contrast, the weight for intensive users with e-mail is 0.71. These households were overrepresented in the sample of completed interviews. Using a weight less than 1.0 gives these observations less weight in the calculation of sample statistics.

Self-Selection Regressions, Tests, and Corrections

An alternative perspective on the problem of response bias is that households self-select whether or not to respond to the survey. Their motivation to respond to the survey is a function of many variables, including the benefits they receive from library services. The econometrics literature addresses the problem of self-selection bias and offers modeling and estimation techniques to address it. We have employed self-selection models and estimation in research using data from our IMLS-sponsored studies and found the models useful. A discussion of these techniques is beyond the scope of this book, but interested research consultants and others will find William Greene's econometrics text and LIMDEP software to be useful resources for this topic.[1]

NOTE

1. William Greene, *Econometric Analysis,* 5th ed. (Upper Saddle River, NJ: Prentice-Hall, 2003). Econometric Software, Inc., *LIMDEP*, Version 8.0, 2002; see http://www.limdep.com.

Technical Insights
for Project Consultants

THIS APPENDIX, WHICH IS INTENDED FOR THE PROJECT'S RESEARCH consultant and survey designer, addresses technical issues and questions regarding our research design and methodology. The appendix is structured to present topics in the context of specific sections of our household and educator survey instruments (refer to appendix C). Topics include modification and use of the survey instruments, validity checks, calculation of consumer surplus, calculation of WTP, and the importance of probes to solicit open-ended responses regarding contingent valuation analysis (CVA) scenarios and answers.

SECTION 1:
HOUSEHOLD CHARACTERISTICS

Section 1 of the household instrument addresses characteristics of the cardholding household and its members' use of library services. Question 1.1 first verifies the household's eligibility for inclusion in the population of active cardholders. Questions 1.1.1 through 1.1.3 explore how members of the household access library services.

Transaction and Travel Costs Associated
with Library Use

Question 1.1.3.1 measures (though crudely) transaction costs for those who travel to the library to use its services. The presumption (verified in our empirical research) is that distance to the library raises the cost of accessing library services and reduces their net value to library users. This component of the study design has several possible applications.

One possible application is branch expansion. With careful crafting in advance, the research consultant could use this type of question in association with respondent addresses to assist the library in estimating the value of adding new branches and in deciding where the new branches should be located.

A second application expands the CBA study outlined here to value the library as a venue for "one-stop shopping" for information. Although the private sector offers many substitutes for services libraries provide, the library offers all of its services under one venue with multiple modes of access. Information seekers may prefer the library to other more limited venues because using one venue saves them time. Economic consultants who wish to address the library's economies of scope should augment question 1.1.3.1 with later queries exploring the library's efficiency in reducing users' transaction cost of acquiring information and materials. See the recent Florida study for an example of this analysis and instrument questions.[1]

Household Characteristics

Questions 1.2 through 1.6 accomplish two objectives. One is to learn more about the household to permit later statistical analysis of library valuation by household characteristics. Note that more sensitive household characteristics such as age, income, and ethnicity are left to the final section of the instrument.

Another objective of this set of questions is to act as a filter. By screening on certain household characteristics, the computerized survey instrument can record default values (zero) for services the household is not likely to use. To reduce the length and complexity of the interview, the instrument also skips questions addressing those services. For example, respondents in households without children need not answer questions about children's services. Only households with members whose primary language is not English answer questions about the library's non-English newspapers and periodicals. The interviewer asks only those households that include a teacher to respond to the educator section of the instrument.

SECTION 2:
HOUSEHOLD'S USE OF LIBRARY SERVICES
AND WILLINGNESS TO SUBSTITUTE

The questions in Section 2 help respondents recall which library services members of their household use, how intensively they use them, and their value to the household. These questions address two objectives in the instrument design.

Reliability

First, Section 2's dialogue between interviewer and respondent about library services prepares the respondent for a later WTP question about the overall value of the library. This WTP question is our most conservative and defensible measure of overall library benefits to the community. The WTP question addressing overall value of library benefits appears in Section 4.

The CVA literature warns that CVA instruments are not reliable unless respondents clearly understand the CVA scenarios and can give carefully considered answers to the CVA question. Surveys that contain redundancies to allow the respondent to think carefully about a topic before answering the WTP question produce more reliable responses.[2]

Our experience is that some dialogue about the household's use of library services is necessary before most respondents can give a considered answer to the CVA question. We employ this strategy for enhancing survey reliability by prefacing the WTP question in Section 4 with our service-by-service exploration of value in Section 2.

For those libraries not wishing detailed service-by-service estimates, the consultant can simplify and shorten Section 2 to prepare the respondent for the CVA question. For example, in the case of books, the interviewer could ask respondents to consider how much more the household would spend per month to purchase books if the library were not there to provide them. Prompt the respondent with ranges of spending. Do the same for other major categories of library service. This abbreviated format helps readers focus on how their household uses the library and the value of its services to the household. The abbreviated format, however, is not likely to provide reliable estimates of the value of individual services.

Calculation of Consumer Surplus

For those libraries interested in detailed service-by-service estimates of benefits, the consultant can use the more structured format of the questions in Section 2. Responses to these questions support the calculation of consumer surplus received by the household for each service used. The methodological argument underpinning these consumer surplus calculations is presented in appendix A.

Below we use the service category "books for adult readers" to illustrate the calculation of consumer surplus for a particular household's use of a library service. From the household survey instrument, the sequence of questions addressing "books for adult readers" is as follows:

> BOOKS1. About how many different books for adult readers do your household members borrow per month from the _____ Library?
>
> BOOKS2. How many books does your household buy per month for its adult readers?
>
> BOOKS3. Suppose that the _____ Library was closed indefinitely due to storm, fire, or earthquake damage and could not provide the books your adult readers want. Also suppose that paperback copies of similar books are available for your household to purchase at a price of <u>BOOKPR</u> each. How many (if any) of the <u>BOOKS1</u> books your household borrows per month from the _____ Library would they replace by purchases at <u>BOOKPR</u> per book?

The response to question BOOKS2 does not figure into the calculation of consumer surplus; it merely serves to ground the respondent for the substitution question in BOOKS3. The calculation of consumer surplus from the library's provision of books borrowed by the household's adult readers is

$$CS = 0.5 \times BOOKPR \times (BOOKS1 + BOOKS3)$$

Some special cases require further consideration, however. What if the household responds that it would not purchase any private-sector substitute service to replace the one used at their library? In this case, the instrument's market price for the substitute service exceeds the household's reservation price. For the sake of conservatism, we have imputed a value of zero benefits for the household's consumer surplus for that particular library service. Clearly, this imputation understates the true value to the household; otherwise, the household would not use the service at all. We argue that this imputation makes our final conclusions from the consumer surplus approach more conservative and defensible.

Technology

One of the areas of service that may be of special interest to libraries is technology. Access to computer hardware, software, the Internet, and electronic databases is important to many different types of library user, from schoolchildren to entrepreneurs. Technology is important to the library's evolving role as an information hub and "one-stop shopping" information venue. Funding agencies such as the Gates Foundation have taken a special interest in this aspect of library service and growth. Nurturing the growth of user value through investment in technology is a critical strategy for libraries who wish to serve their communities well.

Confirm whether or not remote access to electronic services and databases requires a library card number, password, or some other type of registration. If access is completely open, sampling only registered library cardholders is likely to understate drastically the user value of electronic technology and resources. To supplement surveys of cardholders, the consultant and liaison should discuss the possibility of inviting unidentified Web users to complete an electronic instrument addressing the services they use and the value they place on the library.

In questions COMP1 through EREF, our instrument permits the estimation of value associated with households' use of computers, software, instructional classes, and electronic databases. The consultant should tailor these questions to the specific technological services offered by the library under study.

"Technospeak" can quickly confuse and frustrate respondents. Remember that the respondent may not be the household member who actually uses the service. Describe the service in terms respondents can readily understand. Train interviewers to offer prompts to ensure that respondents can identify the service in question.

SECTION 3:
VALIDITY CHECK

Section 3 provides a validity check for the responses in Section 2.

Sum of Consumer Surplus Estimates
Exceeds WTP

In our research, repeatedly we have found that the sum of the consumer surplus estimates across all library services far exceeds the WTP estimate of overall library value using CVA. We have considered several possible reasons for this.

The Whole Is Not the Sum of Its Parts

The CVA literature points out that summing individually measured valuations of attributes or components may yield an aggregate valuation that differs substantially from the WTP respondents place on the whole.[3] There are several possible explanations for this.

QUESTION SEQUENCE

One explanation is that the order in which the services are presented distorts respondents' estimates of value. The order of the valuations matters because respondents may view each additional component as an increment to those presented earlier, making the earliest components more highly valued.

In our computerized survey instruments, we have responded to this concern by randomizing the sequence of services presented to the respondent in Section 2. Yet in our studies using randomized sequencing, WTP is still much larger than the sum of the consumer surplus estimates. Although we believe that the order of services in Section 2 should be randomized to avoid systematic bias in estimating the value of the individual services, randomizing does not appear to address lack of proximity between WTP and the sum of the consumer surplus estimates.

COMPLEMENTS OR SUBSTITUTES

Another explanation is that library services are not separable in the household's utility function but rather are complements or substitutes. If the components are complements, aggregating individual measurements understates WTP for the whole. If components are substitutes, aggregating individual measurement overstates WTP for the whole.[4]

Often library users pick up several books or information sources in the hopes that at least one will satisfy their purpose. If so, library services may be substitutes for each other and aggregation would overstate WTP, as we have found in every library studied.

Some have suggested asking WTP first and then asking respondents to disaggregate WTP to find the value of individual components. We have rejected this strategy in favor of exploring specific services first. This is based on our experience in field tests where respondents expressed the need to ground their thinking first in how the household uses and values specific library services prior to any questions that ask them to value the library as a whole.

BINDING BUDGET CONSTRAINT

Because of the household's budget constraint, all goods and services consumed by the household are substitutes in that consuming more of one has an opportunity cost in terms of consumption of others. As stated above, if the subcomponents are substitutes, then the sum of the subcomponents should exceed WTP for the whole. We doubt that this is the dominant cause of the phenomenon we have observed, however.

BUDGET CONSTRAINT BIAS

A more likely explanation is that respondents exhibit "budget constraint bias."[5] In answering service by service, respondents may not adequately consider the impact of their cumulative replacement spending on their household's budget constraint.

To address this potential bias, we have included a validity check in Section 3. The validity check prompts the interviewer to tell the respondent the cumulative replacement spending implied by their responses to questions from Section 2. Next the interviewer asks if this is an amount the household would truly be willing to commit to such purchases if the library did not exist.

In our studies using this check, many respondents have expressed surprise at the cumulative size of the replacement spending implied by their responses and have chosen to reduce the amounts they are willing to commit. Thus, budget constraint bias appears to be responsible for some of the disparity between WTP and the sum of the consumer surplus estimates. Even after offering this correction, however, substantial disparity has persisted in the final results.

Validity and Interpretation of Benefit Estimates from the Consumer Surplus Approach

As explained above, our empirical work suggests that the service-by-service consumer surplus approach in Section 2 consistently yields cumulative estimates of benefits that exceed the household's overall WTP from the CVA approach. This disparity occurs despite the validation check and correction in Section 3 and the conservative imputation of consumer surplus as zero for those households that choose not to replace some library services.

Consumer Surplus as an Upper Bound to the Library's Value

Because of the disparity in valuations, we have often reported our final estimates of overall benefits as a range. The WTP value provides the lower bound of the range of total general user benefits. The cumulative consumer surplus provides the upper bound of the range. After combining these with estimates of benefits to other types of users, often we offer our conclusion as "The Library provides benefits to the community of at least $xxx per year and possibly as great as $xxx."

Which Is More Valid—WTP or Consumer Surplus?

Although the WTP estimate is lower and hence more conservative, it is not necessarily more accurate. In Section 4 the WTP scenario cites local taxes and fees as the source of library fiscal support. If households discount their WTP responses because of resentment over the payment system in the scenario, then WTP falls short of cumulative consumer surplus. Some would argue that the payment system biases WTP downward. WTP must then understate the actual value of the library to the direct users and the community.

Others would point out that the public library is a community institution reliant on funding through taxes and fees. Hence, consideration of the payment system is integral to the library's valuation. From this perspective, WTP more accurately represents the value of the library to the community and cumulative consumer surplus overstates community benefits.

The public finance literature offers other explanations that may help us understand why our two approaches yield different valuations. Why might goods and services made available by the library as a public agency be valued differently from similar goods and services purchased individually in the private sector? Some of these explanations address the system of revenue supporting the provision of the good or service and some address the production and distribution of the good or service.

First, even though the WTP question states that the library will not exist unless sufficient funds are raised through the referendum, respondents may believe that in such circumstances others would pay anyway to restore the library and continued public access to library services.

Their household could refuse to pay and then "free ride." Maybe they believe that the federal or state government would provide emergency funds to rebuild. Maybe they believe that private donors would step up to fill any funding gap. This is a form of CVA scenario rejection. Households may not admit to this reasoning, even if the interviewer probes. If so, the willingness to pay the household reports in response to the authors' CVA scenario may understate their true valuation of the library and its services. The consumer surplus approach may represent more accurately the household's true valuation.

Second, when paying taxes to fund the library, the household is paying for a collectively available bundle of services determined by a central authority—the library. When purchasing goods or services from private vendors, the household uses its funds for only those purchases that satisfy its own preferences. No funds are expended on services that it doesn't use or value. Furthermore, the household may find utility in physically owning the materials it purchases and creating its own private collections rather than sharing materials collectively through the library. If so, the consumer surplus approach could produce higher estimates of value than the WTP approach.

SECTION 4:
CONTINGENT VALUATION: HOUSEHOLD'S
OVERALL WILLINGNESS TO PAY

Section 4 of the general user survey instrument uses CVA to measure the household's overall willingness to pay. Descriptions of the WTP referendum format using an open-ended question to gauge the respondent's maximum willingness to pay for a public good, including consideration of the property rights issue regarding WTP versus WTA, are available in the literature.[6] Section 4.0 queries the respondent using an open-ended query.

Nevertheless, the CVA literature, including the NOAA panel, clearly regards open-ended WTP queries as less reliable than the "yes" or "no" referendum method.[7] Section 4.1 of our general user survey instrument offers an alternative format for the WTP query that simulates a "yes" or "no" referendum using randomly assigned payment amounts. The referendum is repeated a second time, with the payment in the second referendum contingent on the respondent's first answer.

Section 4.0 WTP Using an Open-Ended Query

Several issues arise in calculating WTP from responses to the open-ended referendum question. Protest votes, hyperbole, and skewness are issues the consultant must address before extrapolating the sample responses to the population of library users.

Protest Votes

Some respondents refuse to offer an amount of taxes or fees their household would be willing to pay support the library. Of these, some simply may not be able to offer a considered, valid response to the question. Others may protest because they perceive the question as an attempt by the library to plan for and promote an increase in their taxes or fees. They simply refuse to cooperate.

Well-trained interviewers could offer prompts to encourage the respondent but must not push the respondent too hard. Forced responses reduce the reliability of the data collected. Instead, the interviewer should follow up with a probe about why the respondent cannot respond. If the issue is one of scenario clarity, the interviewer may be able to add insight that permits the respondent to offer an answer.

Some respondents, however, rather than refuse to answer, respond with an answer of "zero" or "none" as their household's willingness to pay. It is important for the interviewer to follow up with a probe to ascertain what motivated the response. Does the response truly represent the household's willingness to pay? Or is this response a protest against the phrasing of the CVA question?

For example, our CVA question poses a scenario in which the library is destroyed by an uninsurable natural disaster. In follow-up questions, some respondents made it clear that they did not believe a scenario in which the library was uninsured and in which only the library was destroyed. They offered a response of "zero" as a protest against the scenario. Several stated that a library that did not insure itself against natural disasters deserved no tax or other support to rebuild. In such cases, it is not clear how the respondent's household actually values the library. Rather than assume that their willingness to pay is actually zero, treat such answers as nonresponses.

Warm Glow

CVA surveys also encounter respondents who intentionally inflate their stated willingness to pay for public goods such as libraries. The respondents want to perceive themselves as generous and supportive of community causes and want the interviewer and researchers to perceive them that way as well. Just as the "zero" protest votes fail to represent true willingness to pay, inflated open-ended responses bias CBA results also.

One way to check for inflated WTP responses is to see if the stated amount appears to be affordable, given the household's income. For each household, we calculate the ratio of their WTP response to their reported household income. We treat as nonresponses any that result in a ratio that is an unreasonable percentage of the household income.

Skewness and Tails

To extrapolate population willingness to pay from sample willingness to pay, typically the researcher uses a measure of central tendency to represent the sample's willingness to pay by a typical household. Then the researcher multiplies that value by the number of households to find the population's willingness to pay.

How can the researcher prevent extreme values from biasing this calculation? There are several other ways of treating the WTP survey data for extreme values.

One is to sort the WTP responses by magnitude, then disregard responses in the highest and lowest percentiles. By eliminating these extreme values, one can eliminate responses that might bias the sample mean for household willingness to pay.

Alternatively, some researchers use the sample's median willingness to pay rather than mean willingness to pay. This avoids the impact of extreme values on the measure of central tendency. But distributions of WTP responses are often skewed, just as income distributions are. Using median rather mean to represent the typical household's willingness to pay understates the total sample's willingness to pay.

We prefer the other strategies we have discussed: filtering the data with follow-up questions, screening the data with the ratio of WTP to income, and disregarding extreme values.

SECTION 6:
EDUCATORS' VALUATION

Unless the library offers special services to area schools and has a list of teacher contacts, you probably will append the educators' survey to the general user survey as illustrated in appendix C. The educator section of the survey contains a filtering question, a section of queries about which library services the educator uses, and an open-ended WTP question.

The survey asks households to self-identify educators who use the library for their profession. Because the original respondent for the household may not be the educator, the filtering question asks educators to confirm that they use the library to support their professional activities.

The next set of questions is intended to prepare the educator for the open-ended WTP question that follows and concludes the interview. The questions ask the educator to consider carefully a list of services the library offers and to respond whether or not the educator or school would have to replace those services if the library did not exist.

The open-ended WTP question asks the educator how much money per year the school or the educator would have to spend to maintain the quality of education if the public library were closed indefinitely. This question embodies several assumptions: that the educator understands and believes the scenario, that the educator knows the means and cost of replacing the library services, and that the educator accepts the premise that the educator's school or the professional educator individually would in fact pay for the replacement to maintain the quality of education. This last premise may violate the ability-to-pay assumption that underpins willingness to pay in contingent valuation analysis. Future researchers may wish to explore other designs for this question in the CVA survey.

NOTES

1. José-Marie Griffiths, Donald W. King, and Thomas Lynch, *Taxpayer Return on Investment in Florida Public Libraries: Summary Report* (Tallahassee: State Library and Archives of Florida, 2004), available at http://dlis.dos.state.fl.us/bld/roi/pdfs/ROISummaryReport.pdf.

2. See, for example, the discussion of measurement bias due to misspecification of scenarios, especially the question of part-whole bias, in Robert Cameron Mitchell and Richard T. Carson, *Using Surveys to Value Public Goods* (Washington, DC: Resources for the Future, 1989): 246–58, especially 250–52; also see the discussion of reliability enhancement through redundancy, 219.

3. See, for example, the discussion of subcomponent aggregation in Mitchell and Carson, *Using Surveys to Value Public Goods,* 44–47.

4. Mitchell and Carson, *Using Surveys to Value Public Goods,* 46.

5. See, for example, the discussion of budget constraint bias in Mitchell and Carson, *Using Surveys to Value Public Goods,* 253–54.

6. Mitchell and Carson, *Using Surveys to Value Public Goods,* 30–41.

7. Kenneth J. Arrow et al., "Report of NOAA Panel on Contingent Valuation," *Federal Register* 58 (1993): 4601–14.

GLOSSARY

Benefit-cost ratio: benefits from a good, service, or activity divided by the cost of the good, service, or activity; if greater (less) than one, the good, service, or activity is (not) worthy of the resource investment.

Capital purchases: purchases of assets with a long productive life, including buildings, furniture, equipment, and some collections.

Census: survey of an entire population rather than a sample.

Computer-assisted telephone instrument (CATI): computer program that guides the interviewer through branching survey questions based on the responses entered.

Consumer surplus: representation of the monetary value consumers associate with a good or service in excess of any costs they must incur to get it; the difference between the amount of money consumers would be willing to pay for a good or service rather than do without it and the consumers' cost (including price).

Contingent valuation analysis (CVA): economic technique that measures the value an individual places on a good or service; most frequently measured in terms of either willingness to pay (WTP) for a good or service rather than do without it or willingness to accept (WTA) payment to do without the good or service.

Cost-benefit analysis (CBA): economic techniques that measure and compare the monetary value of benefits from a good, service, or activity to the cost of the good, service, or activity; in policy analysis, a formal way of measuring the benefits of alternative public-sector options relative to the cost of those options.

Depreciation: decline in the value of a capital asset.

Direct benefits: benefits from a transaction or activity that accrue to those individuals who are engaged immediately in the activity.

Economic impact analysis: economic study that compares regional economic conditions in the presence of an activity with regional economic conditions in the activity's absence; estimates the change in regional economic indicators, such as income and employment, due to the introduction or loss of the activity.

Existence value: individuals' willingness to pay to support the existence or continuation of something they may never use themselves.

General users: active cardholding households; in the context of CBA methods described in this book, active cardholders who have used their library accounts during the previous twelve months. A cardholding household consists of one or more library cardholders who list the same address.

Indirect benefits: benefits from a transaction or activity that accrue to individuals other than those who are engaged directly in the activity; sometimes called third-party benefits.

Leveraging: matching revenue from one source with additional revenue from another.

Net benefits: benefits less costs.

Non-use benefits: indirect benefits, including existence value and option value, accruing to those who do not use the library themselves.

Option value: individuals' willingness to support the provision of a good or service on the chance that they may want to use it in the future, even though they do not use it today.

Rate of return: fraction, usually expressed as a percentage, in which the numerator represents the net returns (or value of net benefits) and the denominator the asset value or cost.

Service-user matrix: array illustrating the relationship between a library's services and the patron groups that use each of those services.

Stratification: use of strategic nonoverlapping divisions of the population from which separate subsamples are drawn to help ensure that the sample is representative of the population.

Transaction costs: costs in excess of price paid that are borne by consumers when searching for, acquiring, or using a good or service.

User investment: value of time and effort spent by patrons in accessing and using library services; term applied by Griffiths and colleagues in their recent CBA study of the Florida library system.

Willingness-to-accept (WTA): contingent valuation technique in which respondents are asked how much they would require as payment to do without a good or service.

Willingness-to-pay (WTP): contingent valuation technique in which respondents are asked how much they would pay to access, preserve, or receive a good or service rather than do without it.

INDEX

A

address information in cardholder database, 57–60
allocation of resources, 29, 108, 115, 118
alternative scenarios in contingent valuation, 81–82
American Library Association, 121
Americans for Libraries Council, 122
assets. *See* capital assets
audiences for services
  and choice of cost measures, 34
  and outcome measures, 24

B

balance sheets, 95
benefit-cost ratio, 13, 38. *See also* cost-benefit analysis
benefits
  measures of, 18–23
  overstatement of, 36–37
  technical insights on, 166–175
  undervaluation of, 6
bias
  adjusting for, 62, 163–165
  in consumer surplus measurements, 20, 74–75
  in cost measurements, 89–90
  in sample selection, 58, 60
  in survey results, 37
  use of stratification, 61–62
board of directors
  benefits to, 118
  communications with, 40, 111–112
  exclusion from survey, 58, 60
book value of assets, 96

bookstores as comparable service, 20
branch libraries, 105–106
budget allocation, 24
budget for study. *See* costs of study
business users
  customizing survey instrument, 82–84
  identification of, 66
  as studied user group, 18

C

capital assets
  measuring rate of return on, 102–103
  measuring value of, 90, 94–97
  undervaluing, 35, 38
capital campaigns
  benefits of study in, 29
  and cost measures, 34–35, 90
  leveraging donations, 103–104, 113–114
  and value of assets, 90
capital purchases, 90–91
cardholder database
  benefits of study to, 118
  quality of data, 31, 37
  sampling plans, 56–67
cash reserves, 98n2
census surveys, 48
central libraries
  and economic impact analysis, 15
  valuation of, 97
challenge grants, 103, 113–114
children, exclusion from survey, 56–57, 60
chi-square contingency test, 62, 163–165
collections, valuation of, 96, 97
comments or suggestions in survey instrument, 71

communication of results, 111–116
comparison of libraries, applicability of cost-
benefit analysis to, 6, 25
completion rate for interviews. *See* response
rates
computer-assisted telephone interviews, 50
consultants
calculation of benefits, 87
costs of, 32, 51
selection of, 41–42
consumer surplus as measure, 18–20
and benefits of library services, 106
customizing survey instrument, 71–75
and overstatement of benefits, 36–37
technical appendix, 125–126, 168–169
contact lists, 51
contingent valuation
and overstatement of benefits, 36
overview, 21–22
questions in survey instrument, 70–71, 75,
78–82
technical notes, 172–174
cost-benefit analysis
advantages, 1–2, 28–29
disadvantages, 6, 30–32, 122
overview, 9–11
costs, measurement of, 89–98
bias, charges of, 89–90
depreciation, 92–93
operating costs, 90–92
in study design, 33–35
understatement of, 38
costs of study
and decision to do study, 32
survey, 16–17
survey agency, 50

D
database. *See* cardholder database
decision making, tools for, 13
demographics
and library benefits, 108–110
of study libraries, 3
depreciation, 92–93, 95–96, 98n1
design of study, 32–38
choice of simple or detailed study, 33
costs, 33–35
defining results, 35–38
survey strategy, 48–49
detailed study, 33, 34–35
direct benefits
vs. indirect benefits, 11–13

as object of survey, 43
and overstatement of benefits, 36
distribution of library benefits, 104–108
donor investment, 99–102
duplicate records in database, 37, 59

E
economic impact analysis
and overstatement of benefits, 37
uses of, 13–16
educators, surveys of
identification of, 65
strategy for, 48
technical notes, 174
equipment, valuation of, 97
evaluation of study, 117–123
existence value, definition, 12

F
feasibility studies, 40
field testing of survey instrument, 85
filtering the library database, 57–61
friends groups, communication of results to,
112
funding, defense of, 29, 90
funding increases, 114
funding sources, 93–94
fundraising, 113–114
furniture, valuation of, 97

G
"general users," 56–57. *See also* households
governance officials, communication of results to,
111–112
government agencies, 66
grants as source of operating funds, 93. *See also*
fundraising
Guidelines for the Conduct of Research
Involving Human Subjects, 55

H
HAPLR Index ratings, 25, 119
household characteristics, technical notes,
166–167
households
vs. cardholders, 56–57
consumer surplus questions, 72–75
contingent valuation questions, 75–82
identification of library users, 31
sampling program. *See* sampling program
strategies for survey, 48–49

I

income of respondents and valuation of benefits, 108–109
indirect benefits. *See also* direct benefits
 vs. direct benefits, 11–13
 and overstatement of benefits, 36
indirect services to users, 107
information technology department
 capability of study support, 31
 sample instructions for random sampling, 127–131
 sampling procedure, 57
 on study team, 43
Institute of Museum and Library Services (IMLS) and outcomes measurements, 120
insurance appraisals, 96
intangible benefits, 12
interviewers
 academic vs. private, 51
 characteristics of, 49–50
 training, 84–85
interviews, 49–50
inventory of library assets, 96–97
investors, identification of, 66
IT department. *See* information technology department

L

large libraries. *See also* medium-sized and smaller libraries
 census surveys, 48
 choice of user groups, 17, 18
 "willingness to pay" questions, 22
length of survey interview, 49
letter to survey subjects, 70, 85–86
level of detail
 in library services list, 46–47
 in service-user matrix, 44
leveraging donations, 103–104, 113–114
leveraging funds, 34, 90
liaison staff member, 43
library buildings, valuation of, 96–97
library cards, activity level of, 57, 58–59
library records. *See* cardholder database
library services
 distribution of benefits by, 106–108
 selection of, 45–47
library statistics, 119

M

marketing campaigns, 29, 51
media, communication of results to, 112–113

medium-sized and smaller libraries
 choice of user groups, 18, 19
 disadvantages of study, 30
 sample service categories, 19
mission statement, 16, 44
multiple regression analysis, 109–110
multiplier effect, 14
music stores as comparable service, 20

N

New York Public Library, 14–15
non-residents
 and contingent valuation questions, 81
 vs. residents, 58, 60
non-use benefits, 12. *See also* indirect benefits
non-users, 113
not-for-profit agencies, 66

O

online research services as comparable service, 20
operating costs, 90–93
 benefits per dollar of, 102
 vs. capital purchases, 90–91
 supplied by parent body, 91–92
option value, definition, 12
order of survey questions, 47
original value, 96
outcome measures, 24–25

P

patrons, disgruntled, 30
personal information in survey instrument, 71
planned giving, 114
planning, 28–39
 deciding to study, 28–32
 measurement of benefits, 40–53
 scope of study, 32–38
policy implications of study, 5–7
press kits, 112
printing and postage, budgeting for, 51
privacy issues
 guidelines for, 55
 and small numbers of respondents, 5, 105
private market substitutes for library services, 73–74, 76–78
productivity and efficiency model, 119
professionalism of survey agency, 49
promotion of less-used services, 107
public relations
 as benefit of study, 118
 and conservative estimates in study, 98
 and interview experience, 49–50
public service announcements, 112

Q

quantification of benefits, 12

R

random sampling. *See also* sampling program
 difficulties of, 4–5
 and IT department, 31
 protocols for, 64–65
 sample instructions to IT staff, 127–131
rapport with respondents, 70, 71
rate of return
 for library funding, 29
 overstatement in, 38, 95–96
 overview, 34–35
reciprocal borrowing agreements, 60
referendum method of contingent valuation,
 80–81
renters and contingent valuation questions,
 81–82
replacement cost of assets, 96
request for proposal (RFP) for consultant
 economist, 41–42
research methodology, 2–5
 chronology, 2–4
 publications, 4
 reliability and applicability, 4–5
residents vs. non-residents, 58, 60
response rates
 business users, 84
 calculation and reporting of, 87, 159–165
 expectations for, 48
 for interviews, 64–65
 and size of sample, 61
return on investment, 118. *See also* rate of return
return to annual operating funds, 34

S

safe haven, library as, 106
St. Louis Public Library case study, 2–3
sampling program, 56–67. *See also* random
 sampling
 defining users, 56–57
 procedure for, 57–61
 stratification of sample, 61–63
Seattle Public Library, 15
security, costs of, 106
service-user matrix
 construction of, 43–49, 118
 definition, 16
 and outcome measures, 24
 in planning, 33

silver bullet, search for, 121–123
simple study, 33, 34
skeptics about uninsured natural disaster, 81–82
small libraries. *See* medium-sized and smaller
 libraries
sound bite summaries of study, 102, 103, 104,
 105, 110
special collections, valuation of, 96, 97
staff
 appreciation of, 111, 115
 communication of results to, 112
 effects of study on, 1–2, 24–25, 107–108, 115,
 118
 exclusion from survey, 58, 60
 expectations of a cost-benefit analysis, 5–6
 for study team, 42–43
 time commitment to study, 32
statewide library systems and economic impact
 analysis, 15
stewardship of library funds, 29–30, 99–100
stratification of database, 61–63
survey agencies
 costs of, 32, 51
 selection of, 49–51
survey instruments, 69–88
 analyzing results, 87
 customizing, 71–84
 draft from service-user matrix, 47
 field testing, 84–85
 programming, 84
 sample business survey, 150–158
 sample household survey, 132–149
 and service-user matrix, 43–44
 structure of, 69–71
survey strategy, designing, 48–49
surveys, scheduling of, 55

T

tangible benefits, 12
taxpayer support
 measuring benefits of, 24
 rate of return, 99–102
 as source of operating funds, 93
teachers. *See* educators, surveys of
testing of survey instrument, 85
thanking respondents, 87
thanking staff, 111
timeline for study, 51–52. *See also* timing of
 surveys
timeliness in selection of survey agency, 50
timing of surveys, 55

tourism and libraries, 14–15
transaction costs, 23

U

undervaluation of benefits, 6
user groups
    allocation of resources, 29–30
    distribution of benefits to, 104–105
    identification of, 16–18, 54–55
    outcome measures for, 24
    and overstatement of benefits, 36
    selection of, 43–45
    survey strategies for, 49
user investment, 23. *See also* value of time
    measure

V

validity checks, technical notes, 169–172
value of time measure, 22–23
value-added measurements, 119–121
vehicles, valuation of, 97

video rental agencies as comparable service, 20
visual news releases, 112
volunteer respondents in field testing, 85

W

walk-in users, benefits to, 66–67
Web-based surveys, 50
"willingness to accept" (WTA) contingent
    valuation, 21, 75, 78
"willingness to pay" (WTP) contingent valuation
    for business users, 83–84
    and overstatement of benefits, 36
    overview, 21–22
    questions in survey instrument, 70–71, 78–80
    technical notes, 167–168

Y

"yes/no" referendum method of contingent
    valuation, 80–81

Dr. Donald S. Elliott is professor and graduate program director in the Department of Economics and Finance at Southern Illinois University Edwardsville. Currently he teaches courses in business forecasting to undergraduate and graduate students in the School of Business and in managerial economics to MBA students. He received his PhD in economics from the University of Minnesota in 1976.

Dr. Glen Holt is the editor of Haworth Press's *Public Library Quarterly.* He is a regular columnist on library economics in Emerald Press's *The Bottom Line* and a regular columnist for the electronic journal *LLN (Library Leadership Network) Bulletin.* Dr. Holt is a winner of PLA's Charlie Robinson Award (2003) for innovation and risk taking in the profession, and he was a member of the Bertelsmann Foundation's International Network of Public Librarians from 1996 until 2003, developing best practices applicable to libraries worldwide. Dr. Holt was director of St. Louis Public Library from 1987 until 2004 and before that served as a teacher and administrator at Washington University in St. Louis and at the University of Minnesota–Twin Cities campus. He holds a BA from Baker University in Kansas and an MA and PhD from the University of Chicago.

Dr. Sterling W. Hayden is currently serving as vice president for fund development and evaluation with the Area Resources for Community and Human Services in St. Louis, Missouri. He received his EdD from the University of Missouri–Columbia.

Dr. Leslie Edmonds Holt consults with libraries and child-serving agencies. She was the director of youth services at St. Louis Public Library from 1990 to 2004. She taught at the Graduate School of Library and Information Science at the University of Illinois–Champaign. Dr. Edmonds Holt was president of the Association of Library Service for Children. She received the Carroll Preston Baber Award from the American Library Association to support her research on how children use library catalogs. She has done research on how to improve service to middle school students that is the basis for this book. She holds a BA from Cornell College in Iowa, an MA in Library Science from the University of Chicago, and a PhD from Loyola University Chicago.

DISCARD